Advance Praises

"Gary Waters' second book, Coaching Millennials from a Character Perspective, is a must-read for any coach to understand the players they are leading. In today's ever-changing landscape, leadership development and culture are incredibly important in building successful teams. Gary has done a fantastic job capturing those qualities and I highly recommend this book for any coach or leader that strives to have a winning culture and develop outstanding leaders."

–**Matt Painter**, Head Basketball Coach, Purdue University

"This book is truly a breath of fresh air in the world of coaching. Coach Waters' cuts through the myths about this generation and focuses on what truly matters – building character. His perspectives are not only practical but deeply inspiring, offering a roadmap for coaches who want to make a real difference in their players' lives. This book is a must-have for any coach committed to nurturing both character and talent."

—**C. Vivian Stringer**, Former Women's Head Coach, Rutgers University

"The values that Coach Waters instills in his programs are the foundation of his consistent success. His unwavering commitment and positive communication of his core values of faith, character, intuition, strength, intelligence, and learning from the past are timeless life lessons and served him well in his career of coaching millennials."

—**Lee Reed**, Athletic Director, Georgetown University

"The most important things we look for when recruiting student athletes is character and toughness. Some young men come from backgrounds where they have developed great character, and some need a coach to step in and help them grow in that area. I've followed Coach Waters' career for over 20 years, and I always came away impressed with the discipline that his teams displayed. There is no better coach to learn from about the principles of discipline and character development for your athletes of any generation."

—**Earl Grant**, Head Basketball Coach, Boston College University

"Gary Waters' Coaching Millennials from a Character Perspective is a must-read for anyone in the coaching profession. Coach Waters brilliantly captures the essence of mentoring today's athletes, emphasizing character development as the foundation for success on and off the court. His insights are not only timely but essential for building teams that thrive in the modern era. This book is a game-changer."

—**Bill Self**, Head Basketball Coach, University of Kansas

"Coach Waters highlights in "Coaching Millennials from a Character Perspective" the importance of building character, which is crucial for developing not just great players, but great people. His wisdom and experience shine through in this book, making it an invaluable resource for any coach looking to make a lasting impact on this generation."

—**John Calipari**, Head Basketball Coach, University of Arkansas

"Coach Waters understands that character is the cornerstone of success, especially when working with today's young athletes. His approach is insightful, practical, and rooted in values that build strong teams and even stronger individuals. 'Coaching Millennials from a Character Perspective' is extremely beneficial for anyone serious about coaching and mentoring the next generation."

—**Kelvin Sampson**, Head Basketball Coach, University of Houston

"Gary Waters' Coaching Millennials from a Character Perspective is a game-changer for anyone looking to truly understand and inspire the Millennial generation. His blend of real-world coaching experience and deep insights into generational dynamics offers a fresh, practical approach that is both empowering and transformative. This book isn't just about coaching—it's about building character, bridging generational divides, and unlocking the full potential of young leaders. A must-read for coaches, managers, and anyone committed to developing the next generation of talent."

—**Tommy Kyle**, Executive Director, Nations of Coaches

"Knowledge, wisdom and experience are the hallmark foundations of teaching and sharing. In this newest book by Gary Waters, you will extract the key components to firsthand experiences, accompanied by real life examples of understanding the next generation and those to come. Many will say that athletics is a microcosm of life, and Coach Waters 40 plus years of coaching experience, couple with research and knowledge, will bring you tangible understanding to help you navigate the challenges of leading multigenerational players and employees. This book is a roadmap to reaching players, but also a vital read for leaders in all areas. It is a must read."

—**Larry DeSimpelare**, Crossroads League Commissioner

"Coach Waters is an insightful, charismatic and servant leader who has spent his life pouring into young men. His unique perspective gained from decades of interacting with millennials has provided him with a front row seat into the minds of this critical generation. "Coaching Millennials from a Character Perspective" is a handbook for serving and inspiring young people."

—**Tim Duncan**, Senior Deputy, Athletic Director,
University of Memphis

"Gary Waters' Coaching Millennials from a Character Perspective is a game-changer for anyone who believes in the power of mentorship beyond the court. As someone who has worked extensively with top athletes and coaches, I understand the importance of building a foundation of character and integrity in sports. Coach Waters masterfully blends his years of coaching experience with a unique approach to developing young talent, offering insights that are both timely and timeless. This book is essential reading for coaches, educators, and leaders who aim to inspire the next generation with principles that last a lifetime."

—**Dennis Coleman**, Sports & Entertainment Attorney,
Ropes & Gray LLP

"Coach Waters is one of the most respected coaches ever to walk the sidelines. In his recently published book "Coaching Millennials from a Character Perspective", he talks about the key principles to successful coaching in the 21st century. As a current coach there are many themes he touches on that are relevant to the student athletes of today. This book is a must read for anyone committed to coaching and leading this talented generation."

—**Steve Pikiell**, Head Basketball Coach, Rutgers University

COACHING MILLENNIALS

from a

CHARACTER PERSPECTIVE

GARY WATERS

Published by Gary Waters, LLC.

www.CoachGaryWaters.com

Scripture quotations taken from The Holy Bible, New International Version® NIV°

Copyright © 1973, 1978, 1984, 2011 by Biblica, Inc." Used by permission of Zondervan. All rights reserved worldwide. www.zondervan.com

ISBN: 979-8-9922036-0-8

ISBN: 979-8-9922036-1-5 eBook

Front cover image courtesy University of Rutgers (Sports Information Department).

TABLE OF CONTENTS

Dedication

This book is dedicated to our grandchildren, with special recognition to our Millennial grandchildren, whom we affectionately call our Grand Millennials. Alexia, Emajae, Bryce, and Jessica represent the Millennial generation, while Gabrielle, Bailey, and Cameron are a part of Generation Z. These seven remarkable individuals have taught my wife, Bernadette, and me the value of intergenerational connection, reminding us to stay curious and engaged with the ever-evolving world they navigate.

Through them, we've learned to embrace technology as a bridge rather than a barrier, keeping our minds and hearts open to their way of seeing and being. Because they are not shy in expressing their opinions, we've learned to listen to and value their voices, even when they differ from ours, and we celebrate the courage of their convictions.

To our Grand Millennials, we pray that each of you find your unique path to connect with the Lord, that you discover the joy of serving and blessing others, and that as you mature, your character continues to grow stronger and shine brighter. We are immensely proud, not just of what you've done, but of who you are and who you are becoming.

You are the living legacy of our values, and we thank you for not only illuminating our lives, but for being the light that shines throughout all generations.

FOREWORD

It was April 6, 2006, the spring before my senior season playing basketball at Cleveland State University. My teammates and I had just found out our new head coach would be Gary Waters from Rutgers University.

As a student of basketball, I already knew a bit about Coach Waters - that he was from Michigan like me, had success coaching at Kent State, and had coached Quincy Douby at Rutgers. Up to that point, he had an impressive coaching resume. However, I still felt uncertain about the coaching change.

Shortly after the announcement, our athletic director, Lee Reed, called me into his office. He asked how I was doing and if I had heard the news.

"Yes, and honestly I don't know how I feel right now," I said.

"Well, do you know who he is, what he's about?"

"I know he's from Michigan and was the head coach at Kent State and Rutgers," I said. Lee smiled and said, "You're right, Vic—he's a Michigan guy who coached at Kent and Rutgers, but there's so much more to this man. This is going to be great for you guys and the program, trust me. I just need you to help get the other guys on board." Though unsure, I hesitantly agreed.

I was born on September 1, 1985, in Shreveport, Louisiana, which makes me a Millennial. I was raised by my mother and spent a lot of time with my grandparents in Minden, Louisiana, until I moved to Inkster, Michigan, when I was 11 years old. My grandmother, a Baby Boomer, my mother a Gen Xer, instilled in me the values of hard work, dedication, loyalty, and respect for elders, and it was these same values that made me skeptical of the coaching change. I was torn. I was loyal to and grateful for the previous coach and staff, who had given this tough kid from Inkster the opportunity to pursue his dreams.

The next day, we met Gary Waters, whom we nicknamed GW. He spoke passionately about changing the culture, letting God lead, pursuing excellence, and even winning championships. His swagger and vision quickly won me over along with the rest of the team. We were sold and ready to work.

Over the course of the next year, the foundation was laid for something special. GW brought in key transfers who would complement our already talented returning athletes. Practices were competitive and intense, pushing each of us to elevate our game. As a senior, I was playing the best basketball of my career before unfortunately suffering a season-ending foot injury.

It was during this challenging time that GW's exceptional character truly shone through. Despite my setback, he remained a constant source of encouragement and support throughout the months of grueling rehabilitation. His belief in my abilities and genuine care for my wellbeing left a lasting mark on me.

My playing career eventually led me overseas, and the experiences and challenges I encountered while traveling around the globe prepared me for my next career, coaching. GW's conduct, both on and off the court, had set the standard for how I should carry myself. His commitment to character and integrity became the bedrock of my coaching philosophy, and I soon found out firsthand how much I would need it.

A lot had changed with respect to the mindsets and attitudes of younger student-athletes, Gen Z to be exact. They had grown up in an era of technology, and were unapologetically opinionated, wanting to be heard and willing to debate. They expected instant results versus gradual rewards through hard work. They're fun and open to being coached once you show and they know that you care about more than just their performance. This is completely different from back in my day—we respected the coach and worked for the coach…because he was the coach.

After a year, GW hired me on staff at Cleveland State. It was shocking and disheartening to witness some of the new attitudes. Entitlement and expectations had reached new heights, with players demanding luxuries beyond traditional scholarships and basic necessities. However, GW handled these egos with integrity and character, always staying true to his principles. I followed suit, striving to build relationships with the players based on respect, support, and mutual growth.

The lessons I learned from Gary Waters about leadership and navigating the generational landscape have been invaluable. He understood that success requires connecting with each player individually and possessed the ability to adapt his coaching style to each generation he worked with, respecting their backgrounds and personalities without ever compromising his character.

Whether you're a coach, leader, parent, or anyone navigating the complexities of intergenerational relationships this book, filled with insights and practical advice, is a must-read. You'll be surprised and empowered by what you discover about yourself, your generation, and the generations that follow, and the incredible potential that arises when we bridge the gaps between us.

—Victor Morris
Former Assistant Coach and Cleveland State Basketball Player

INTRODUCTION

During my last fifteen years of coaching college basketball, I witnessed firsthand the profound impact of the Millennial generation on the coaching profession. In 2001, as I embarked on my 32nd year of coaching, I found myself at Rutgers University, eager to navigate the evolving landscape.

Having spent the previous five years leading the Kent State Basketball program to remarkable success while instilling a culture rooted in character, I understood the importance of molding young minds. However, as the times were changing in college basketball, I realized that my approach needed to adapt. The players I encountered at Rutgers would be the last cohort accustomed to unflinchingly following instructions without questioning authority.

A new generation was emerging, one with an entirely different value system. As a coaching staff, my colleagues and I were faced with the challenge of guiding and inspiring this unique group of talents, whose lives and thinking were greatly shaped by social media and electronic technology. These young adults, commonly known as Millennials or Generation Y, were born between 1984 and 2002, give or take a few years in either direction.

The younger Millennials, born after 1990, displayed both similarities and stark contrasts compared to their earlier Gen Y counterparts. Notably, they were heavily influenced by technology, earning them the moniker "Generation iY." Tim Elmore, in his book, *Generation iY – Our Last Chance to Save Their Future,* aptly captures the impact of the internet on their lives. Their world revolves around devices like iPhones, iPads, and previously iPods, and their lives often center around the concept of "I." They are generally less rebellious and more tolerant, but they are also less happy and unprepared for adulthood.

Despite their reliance on technology, as Elmore points out, Millennials can be energetic, confident, and capable. They dream big, care about their friends, and thrive on activity. To be clear, these characteristics do not apply universally to all individuals born between the mid-eighties and early two-thousands.

As time progressed, a new generation emerged, known as Generation Z or the Post-Millennials. Born in 1995 or later, they were born into a world overrun with technology and face even higher expectations and demands. They are less focused but can process information faster than other generations. They have shorter attention spans but can efficiently shift between work and play, handling multiple tasks simultaneously.

One significant difference with Generation Z is their value of independence and their ability to learn non-traditionally. They are expected to have a considerable impact on culture in the near future, as they already make up more than a quarter of the U.S. population and will soon account for 40% of the nation's consumers.

But Generation Z aside, my focus lies primarily on Millennials in this book, as they significantly influenced my coaching and leadership. They played a pivotal role in shaping the foundation I established during my later years in the basketball profession. And though they had a markedly different mindset than the players I'd coached previously, I remained committed to incorporating faith and character building into their growth and development, believing that these elements went hand-in-hand. Despite the challenges of reaching this generation, I found great fulfillment in engaging with them once they became invested in the process.

Coaching these Millennials often felt akin to working in an Emergency Room (ER), where the balance of players' future rested in my hands as I navigated crucial decisions. This metaphor will be recurrent throughout the book, drawing parallels between the chaos of the ER and the behavior of this generation. Unexpectedly, writing this book itself became a transformative experience for me as a form of Millennial transformation emerged within.

Steven A. Smith

On most days, I would retreat to a secluded room, seeking an undisturbed environment to immerse myself in the completion of the book. Alongside my necessary materials, I would often turn on the television to a recorded episode of the "First Take" program. As I listened and occasionally glanced at the debates between renowned sports commentators Steven A. Smith and Max Kellerman, moderated by Molly Qerim on ESPN, I found my attention divided among multiple stimuli. Though I intended to focus solely on the task at hand—the writing of the book—I couldn't help but become distracted by the surrounding commotion.

Initially, I considered this to be a form of multitasking, a skill that Millennials believe they have mastered. However, I came to realize that it wasn't true multitasking at all. Brain researchers suggest that true multitasking doesn't exist; instead, what we perceive as multitasking is actually "mental juggling" or "rapid toggling" between tasks. In other words, we are not truly performing two tasks simultaneously, but rather switching back and forth between them. According to Simon Sinek in his book "Leaders Eat Last," our brains require time to reset and refocus each time we switch tasks. Thus, multitasking not only fails to enhance speed or efficiency but actually hinders productivity. The American Psychological Association further asserts that shifting between tasks can consume up to 40 percent of our productive time.

Interestingly, I found that the players of this generation often believe they can draft a document on a computer, listen to music or a television in the background, and engage in a FaceTime conversation with a friend on their iPhone or iPad—all simultaneously. This multitasking approach becomes their way of performing. However, researchers argue that those who believe they are more productive through multitasking are mistaken. In reality, they are simply better at being distracted, as Simon Sinek explains in his work.

As I delved deeper into this book, my aim was to shed light on a seldom-discussed aspect of Millennial growth and development: character. As their coach, it was my responsibility to lead by example and provide my

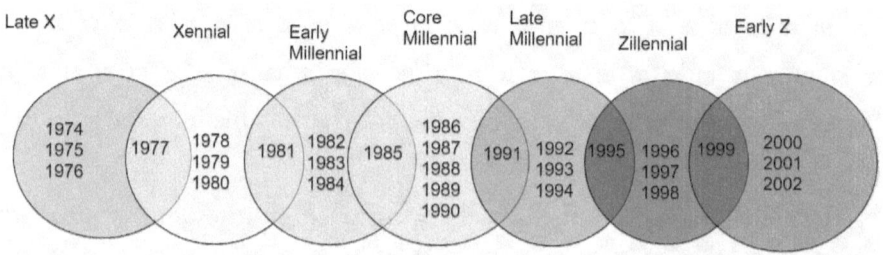

players with the tools to bridge the gap between their generation and those that came before, fostering greater productivity, which is the same bridge

Past generations, such as the Baby Boomers and Generation X, integrated character development into their daily lives, while Millennials often viewed it as an attack on their character. This divergence perpetuated a continuous separation between generations, explored throughout the chapters in various situations. Each chapter examines how Millennial individuals navigated a constantly changing environment and coped with authority figures whose perspectives they struggled to comprehend. The frustration and misunderstanding were mutual, as older generations found it challenging to relate to and understand the younger generation's way of thinking.

This miscommunication extended beyond the basketball court to homes, relationships, and classrooms, illustrating the limited control and cooperation Millennials experienced in various aspects of their lives. Yet, many of the negative behavioral traits attributed to this generation could be distortions of the truth of who they really are. Through this book, I aim to challenge misconceptions and present an alternative perspective that showcases the multifaceted nature of Millennials.

So, join me as we dribble up and down the basketball court and navigate the halls of the Emergency Room, encountering pressures from parents, identity crises, distractions, expectations, and communication gaps. Together, let us explore how character building can serve as a bridge, connecting generations in our ever-changing world.

Chapter 1:

DISTINCT IDENTITY

"Never forget who you are, for surely the world will not. Make it your strength. Then it can never be your weakness. Armour yourself in it, and it will never be used to hurt you."

—**George R.R. Martin**, American Novelist
(A Game of Thrones)

Completing our fifth and final year at Kent State in 2001 marked the end of a championship season and the dawn of a new horizon. Kent State served as the birthplace of my career as a head coach at the NCAA Division 1 level, and those five years were incredibly successful. However, it was the fifth season that stood out as the most rewarding. We emerged victorious, clinching both the Mid-American Conference (MAC) regular season championship and the post-season tournament championship, which earned us a coveted NCAA Tournament bid.

During the NCAA Tournament's opening round, we achieved one of the biggest upsets in its history by defeating the sixth-ranked University of Indiana. Our remarkable run came to an end in the regional finals against the University of Cincinnati, led by Hall of Famer Bobby Huggins. This achievement was even more remarkable considering we accomplished it with first-generation Millennials, who were only just beginning to

KSU Championship

understand the concept of their generational label.

These early Millennials at Kent State were distinct from the stereotype of the "Me First" and "I before Team" mentality often associated with their generation. They didn't receive trophies just for participation or praise for completing routine tasks. Instead, they embodied honor and a strong work ethic. Their character was shaped by their parents or grandparents, who were trailblazers in facing adversity. They tackled challenges and pressure head-on, prepared to manage any emergency, much like attentive hospital staff.

However, as Malcolm Harris explains in his book *Kids These Days,* this unique group of Millennials soon became a fading breed. Throughout the remainder of my coaching career, I only encountered glimpses of their exceptional traits in a few individuals from subsequent generations. The landscape was changing, giving rise to a new class of young competitors born between 1984 and 2002, or even as early as 1980, depending on researchers' classifications.

Their focus centered on themselves and survival in a world where technology had taken center stage in their education. Conflicting descriptions emerged about this generation. Some characterized them as lazy, narcissistic, delusional, coddled, and entitled, while others saw them as open-minded, confident, self-expressive, liberal, upbeat, and receptive to new ideas and lifestyles.

In *Generation iY,* Tim Elmore describes Millennials as "a generation of paradox; sheltered yet pressured, self-absorbed yet generous, social yet isolated by technology, ambitious yet anxious, adventuresome yet protective, and high achievers yet high maintenance." These descriptions may ring true or be misrepresentations of this complex Millennial generation.

Personally, as I delved deeper into understanding this generation, I uncovered more information that revealed additional layers to their identity. While the upperclassmen I presently coached at Kent State were not yet influenced by this transformative thinking, I knew that our incoming freshmen had already begun to exhibit this new behavior.

The formation of their new identity sparked a surge of questions they had never contemplated before. No longer content with accepting the status quo, they boldly began to ask "why" and challenge conventional wisdom. It is this spirit of inquiry and defiance that led to the alternate moniker for Millennials—Generation Y.

Bobby Knight

This transformation reached far beyond their personal lives; it even extended to questioning the coaching methods employed on the basketball court. Such an approach was deemed taboo by the old-school coaches. Even legendary figures like Bobby

Knight, renowned for his coaching prowess in college basketball, found himself questioning his methodologies and introspecting. Perhaps it was this evolving mindset that led to his unexpected departure from the game he had mastered.

However, as this generation was only in the early stages of its maturation, this newfound way of thinking had not yet influenced the upperclassmen I presently coached at Kent State. They still had one more year before graduation. Nonetheless, I recognized the urgency to enhance my knowledge and understanding of this generation in order to connect with our upcoming recruiting class. The wave of change had already begun to infiltrate the group of entering freshmen, much like how it permeated the Millennials I cherished and was closely connected to.

Grandson Bryce Allen

This mindset also began to affect the Millennials I was close to and loved. I recall a poignant incident involving my wife and our grandson, Bryce Allen, which shed light on this prevailing Millennial mindset. My wife had taken Bryce to the voting polls for the first time, an activity he seemed reluctant to partake in. While waiting in line to cast their ballots, a heated conversation about voting rights ensued between my wife and our grandson. Bryce expressed skepticism, stating, "It doesn't matter if we vote or not because the ones in control will manipulate the outcome anyway. So, why am I here voting in the first place?"

Stunned by his remark, my wife responded by reminding him of the sacrifices made by countless individuals who had fought and given their lives to secure the opportunity and right to vote. Her words resonated not only with Bryce but also with the elderly women in their late seventies standing behind them. In the tear-filled eyes of one of those women, my wife witnessed the weight of personal loss and the profound significance of civic participation.

Moved by the conversation, the second woman addressed our grandson, saying, "She is right. My son served in the military and lost his life so that you could have this right. I am disappointed that you feel this way." This incident reinforced my belief that this Millennial way of thinking must be guided and nurtured to help their generation understand their identity, recognize the struggles of those who came before them, and acknowledge the individuals who paved the way for their present freedoms.

This type of attitude and approach became apparent during early recruiting visits when the student-athletes took control of the narrative, while their parents asked fewer questions. While initially this appeared impressive, it also signaled a shift towards a more self-centered mindset, with less regard for parental involvement.

As a coach, I recognized that my job would become more challenging, and the focus on character development would be even more crucial for this generation. Once the basketball season was over, however, I faced a new challenge: venturing into a different environment full of millennials. I left my post at Kent State University and took the job of head coach at Rutgers University in the Big East Conference, the top NCAA Division 1 college basketball league.

This move was motivated by various factors, including the challenges presented by the Millennial Generation. The decision to leave a mid-major conference for a pressure-oriented program in an unfamiliar environment highlighted the significance of this generational shift.

THE EMERGENCY ROOM SAGA BEGINS

What started out as a regular morning ended with a traumatic experience in the Emergency Room (ER) of a Tampa, Florida area hospital during the month of January in 2019. On the 17th, I woke up with abdominal pain and bleeding, so I called my primary care doctor's office, who then recommended that I go to the nearest ER at the Tampa General System.

My wife had already left for her own appointment, so I was on my own for the thirty minute drive. Parking wasn't easy either; there was only one public parking structure located far from the facility. After trekking to the entrance, I was shocked by how many people were inside going in different directions.

Five arduous hours elapsed before I finally met with an experienced doctor. During this ordeal, I encountered numerous nurses and attendants who attended to me but provided no definitive results. It became evident to me why the healthcare industry had experienced escalating financial burdens. Amidst the chaos, the first individual who offered genuine assistance was an elderly receptionist, I deduced she was of the Baby Boomer generation. Her willingness to navigate the abnormality and chaos of the ER made me realize that enduring a lengthy waiting period was inevitable due to the overcrowding and the multitude of individuals seeking medical attention for their emergencies.

After seeing the receptionist, I was directed to the waiting room where people were so close together, it felt like they were practically on top of each other. Two young attendants loudly discussed the fate of an elderly patient without considering their feelings or attempting to filter their conversation. They said something along the lines of "It doesn't matter if she's in the ER, because there's nothing we can do for her anyway - she's too old." I realized this was just another example of how Millennials view older generations as less relevant, perhaps due to their perceived antiquated views and ways of thinking.

Sitting in that waiting room, witnessing the diverse range of reactions from those around me, shed new light on the challenges I would face during my first year at Rutgers University. It dawned on me that this generation, the Millennials, was unlike any other. They stood alone in their thinking, which permeated every aspect of their lives.

"They dream big, care about their friends, and thrive on activity," says Tim Elmore in *Generation iY.* This makes it crucial for them to connect with the older generation and gain the wisdom needed to navigate these thought-provoking times successfully.

As I reflected upon this experience, I could not help but anticipate the unique challenges and revelations I would encounter while coaching players in this new environment in Piscataway, New Jersey. If this episode is even remotely comparable to what lies ahead, I am truly in for an extraordinary journey as I strive to understand and embrace the distinct identity of this generation.

In the chapters to follow, I delve deeper into this generational shift and explore the impact it had on my coaching journey at Kent State. It is my belief that by understanding the unique mindset of this rising generation, we can forge meaningful connections, bridge generational gaps, and ultimately inspire growth and success both on and off the basketball court.

Chapter 2:

PARENT PRESSURE

"Pressure of parents on one side, pressure of studies on the other and some other pressures too . . . life is like a pressure cooker without any safety valve."

—Somnath Mukherjee, Managing Partner & CIO of Bloomberg Quit

My decision to leave Kent State was met with mixed emotions; while many saw my ambition and wished me success, others felt hurt by the coming changes. Even though most knew that, eventually, I would soar to greater heights leaving this haven in my rearview. The results we achieved in a very short time had grabbed the attention of those who held higher positions, greater aspirations, as well as high values. Albert Einstein aptly summed it up when he said, "Try not to become a man of success, but rather try to become a man of values."

When I arrived at Rutgers, I had no preconceived expectations, apart from knowing their beautiful campus made them an ideal recruiting base due to its proximity to New Jersey and New York. Every coach knows how essential recruiting is to any successful program—it's the lifeblood.

I accepted the offer extended by Rutgers University with trepidation as I headed back to campus to tell my players and staff about my decision. To part ways with people who I had developed, nurtured and loved for five years was difficult. As tears welled up in our eyes, we shared our heartbreak for an hour. To my surprise, they were just as excited at my opportunity as I was! Not only that, their parents showed me appreciation beyond what I could have anticipated.

Gary Waters at Press Conference

But in all honesty, this group of parents were also a dying breed. Their expectations for their children were high and uncompromising. They wanted them to not only work hard in school and excel on the basketball court, but also respect authority and conduct themselves with immense character. Different from the new-age parents, they had raised their first-generation Millennials to respect those who were older than them and understand that success would never be achieved without effort. This conglomeration of talented student-athletes understood my dedication to their development and worked hard to become exemplary role models for future generations.

This left me with an urgent question: why would I leave such a successful program for what seemed like greener pastures? We had worked together to build something remarkable, creating a culture based on values and shaping talented young men into positive role models. Could this latest generation be an extension of their parents' passion? Why walk away from all this? The obvious reasons would be fame, money and prestige.

But my character would not accept those superficial career attainments of success to supplant my personal values. I had already decided before I entertained the offer from Rutgers, if I were approached by a university that met certain criteria, I would be willing to consider it.

These criteria were straightforward: the university had to be in a high-profile Division 1 conference, have high media visibility, and possess a high-level recruiting base within a 50-mile radius from the campus. Rutgers met all three criteria, which enticed me to take my talents to New Jersey, and the rest became history. While the money and challenge were appealing, my decision to leave Kent State was based solely on these three criteria.

Upon my arrival at Rutgers, I made the decision to bring my entire coaching staff with me, which turned out to be a deterrent in a foreign environment, but having them with me provided some comfort in navigating the unfamiliar setting. It was important to have my trusted team by my side as we prepared to face the challenges posed by the new generation of athletes we would encounter at Rutgers University. Unfortunately, these first-year Millennials had already endured significant damage from their prior interactions with the previous coaching staff. They had been subjected to verbal abuse and mistreatment, leaving them wounded and in need of support to heal their emotional distress.

EMERGENCY ROOM SAGA CONTINUES . . .

This situation brought me back to that day in the emergency room, where I witnessed the urgent needs of patients seeking relief. In the crowded waiting room, I heard people in severe pain crying out for help, their suffering seemingly endless. Wheelchairs filled with individuals who had lost limbs or were paralyzed were scattered throughout the room. It felt reminiscent of a wartime military hospital, reminiscent of the television show "M*A*S*H" from the late seventies.

I had to have blood drawn at the lab, and even that area was overcrowded and understaffed. They took me there as a gesture to compensate for the long wait. The male nurse who performed the blood draw was a Millennial, seemingly unaware of the chaos unfolding in the trauma ward. He complained incessantly about being overwhelmed by the elderly patients. One person was in such excruciating pain that the other patients in the room pleaded for her to be moved to the front of the line. It was a sight that left a lasting impression.

Returning to the situation with the team at Rutgers, I recognized the need to bring in someone who could help uncover the hidden scars and trauma that these young men had experienced. I hired Dr. Joseph Carr, a board-certified clinical sports psychologist and from Washington, D.C. I received a strong recommendation for Dr. Carr from Ben Braun, the head basketball coach at the University of California, Berkeley. Ben and I had worked together at Eastern Michigan for eight years, sharing a similar ideology. Several high-profile programs were already utilizing Dr. Carr's services, further affirming his expertise.

While I had some familiarity with the role of sports psychologists based on previous experiences with team building, these circumstances demanded a specialist who could delve deep into the minds of these hurting Millennials.

I had a partial understanding of the trauma and issues they had gone through, but I was curious to learn about the specific pressures they faced. In Dr. Carr's early sessions, he uncovered surprising and deeply troubling pressures that stemmed from their parents or guardians. It was astonishing to discover that over half of the players in the program were raised by single parents. Regardless of the type of parenting, the pressures they experienced were ones I had not fully realized—the pressures exerted by those who were supposed to love and care for them, responsible for their well-being.

Dr. Carr

In Simon Sinek's book *Leaders Eat Last*, he references Julie Lythcottt-Haims, a former Stanford dean and author of *How to Raise an Adult*. "All that over-parenting has also made many of them (Millennials) desperately afraid of failure and uncertain how to handle conflict or setbacks. 'They seem to be scanning the sidelines for Mom and Dad,' she writes, unable to cope with normal ups and downs of life." This resonated with what I was observing in some of the Millennials I was currently coaching.

Dr. Carr's sessions revealed that a few of these individuals had been subjected to constant pressure and criticism for quite some time. Their parents expected them to attend college and earn a degree, projecting their own achievements or failures onto their children. Despite some experts suggesting that a college education is not always necessary for success, the relentless demands from their parents had taken a toll on the mental well-being of these young Millennials.

Nevertheless, they were compelled to continue down this path, regardless of their own desires. In order to participate in the sport they loved, they had to maintain eligibility and work towards a degree—a requirement set by the university. Additionally, there were parents who saw their child as a means to advance their own ambitions.

Malcolm Harris, in his book *Kids These Days: Human Capital and the Making of Millennials*, argues that this generation has been burdened with excessive homework and extracurricular activities, all in the name of preparing for college and successful careers. However, it often leads to the inevitable disappointment of falling short of both their parents' and their own expectations. Consider the immense pressure these Millennials were facing, yet they managed to maintain their sanity.

As the season progressed, I noticed signs of low self-esteem, increasing unhappiness, and reduced productivity in certain aspects of their lives, as discussed by Sinek in *Leaders Eat Last*. These negative effects even spilled over into their beloved sport, basketball. However, I also discovered that they became more creative and inspired when fully engaged in the process of whatever they were trying to accomplish.

Furthermore, I observed that these Millennials were unafraid to showcase their moral compass once I connected with their inner being, their true selves. It became evident that they craved meaningful connections, especially when they witnessed the shortcomings of the system they lived and worked in, which did not meet their expectations. During such times, they relied on the moral beliefs instilled in them by their parents, seeking guidance from their core values.

As a coaching staff at Rutgers, our commitment was to recruit morally driven student-athletes. Tim Elmore, in his book *Generation iY,* refers to this as 'Moral Intelligence.' According to Elmore, we need to guide Millennials towards robust character, including personal discipline, a secure sense of self, and strong positive values. These qualities are more important than the traditional metrics society typically focuses on, such as GPA, SAT or ACT scores, or IQ rankings.

To assess this generation at Rutgers, we dedicated most of our time to getting to know and understand these Millennials. The more we connected with them, the better we grasped the stressors they faced and the immense pressure exerted by their parents. Society has even assigned labels to the parents of this generation, highlighting their level of involvement.

Elmore also asserts that we not only have a new generation of kids but also a new generation of parents who are committed to controlling their children's lives. Among the damaging parenting styles we encountered at Rutgers, helicopter parents were prominent. These parents constantly hovered over their children, being controlling and obsessive in their efforts to ensure everything goes perfectly for them, shielding them from negative incidents that might affect their self-esteem or prospects.

However, this approach denies children the opportunity to learn from failure and persevere. As Frank A. Clark stated, "The most important thing that parents can teach their children is how to get along without them," as cited in *Generation iY.*

Another parenting style we encountered was that of Karaoke parents. These parents hungered to be buddies with their children and emulated the behavior of the younger generation. They often failed to provide clear boundaries that promote security and self-esteem, prioritizing being liked over being respected. Additionally, they tended to idolize their children and place them on a pedestal.

We also encountered Groupie parents who treated their children like celebrities, viewing them as 'stars' to be honored and served, catering to their every whim. Unfortunately, they failed to recognize their role as stewards entrusted with raising their children to become mature, contributing adults who give back to society.

The Commando parent, a military-style parenting approach, was becoming less prevalent in this generation, and we encountered fewer instances of this style at Rutgers. This parenting style, although well-intentioned, could be damaging by prioritizing rules over building a relationship with the child, as Elmore explains.

Rutgers Parent Orientation

While there are many other parenting styles assigned to the parents of Millennials, the ones I mentioned were the types we frequently encountered at Rutgers. It became our responsibility not only to mentor and guide the young adults we were coaching but also to establish a rapport with their parents and understand the various parenting approaches our players experienced. Parental pressure had become ingrained in how this generation performed at the collegiate level, and as leaders, we needed to be aware of it.

Chapter 3:

CREATING RELATIONSHIPS

"Relationships are harder now because conversations become texting, arguments become phone calls, and feelings become status updates."

—**Bandile Mnisi,** Founder of Birdie Podcast Agency

When my staff and I arrived on the eastern coast, we had no prior connections or acquaintances in the New Jersey and New York area. This region felt as foreign to us as another country, given the differences in people, language, and surroundings compared to the Midwest. The unfamiliar territory presented a challenge unlike any other for a college coach. It took us three years to establish meaningful relationships and break into this tough, dominating environment.

At the time, it was probably one of the most intimidating settings for recruitment and coaching in the country. This challenge was compounded by a generational shift, as everyone involved ventured into what I call a "New Millennium," a completely different way of doing things. But we were determined to crack into this new era and connect with the Millennial generation players who made up our team. We needed to uncover their true competitive nature and gain their trust as the coaches leading them into this new era.

We inherited an entirely new team, with eight returning players from the previous year's roster and the rest being incoming freshmen or transfers from other programs. Despite their diverse backgrounds, they all shared one commonality: they belonged to the Millennial generation and had a similar thought process. Our task as a staff was to uncover their true competitive nature and gain their trust as the coaches leading them into this New Millennium.

Out of the entire team, only one player, Jerome Coleman, had a prior connection with our staff. We had recruited him from junior college in Northeast Maryland, and he was the sole addition to our program that year. Jerome had an impressive track record, being a junior college All-American honorable mention and one of the top three-point shooters in the junior college ranks. Our program desperately needed his shooting ability, as we only had one returning player who could shoot three-pointers, and he hadn't played a single minute the previous season.

During his two years at Rutgers, Jerome emerged as one of the top three-point shooters in the Big East. After graduation, he went on to have a successful career overseas for eight years. It was fortunate that Jerome had a pre-existing relationship with one of the returning players, Mike Sherrod, which helped facilitate interactions within the team.

Mike and Jerome had played together at Roberson High School in Brooklyn, New York, and had developed a close bond over the years. Mike had an outstanding freshman season at Rutgers, earning him a spot on the Big East All-Freshman team.

The incoming freshmen class that year was recruited by the former staff and had a standout player leading the group named Ricky Shields from Marlboro, Maryland. Ricky had finished his high school career at Hargrave Military Academy in Chatham, Virginia. He was highly

regarded, even earning a spot in the McDonald's All-American game. Ricky was an exceptional athlete with a consistent 3-point shot, making him a valuable asset. He turned out to be the gem of the freshmen class, earning recognition as an All-Freshman Big East performer in his first season.

Ricky Shields

Among the other freshmen, Jewell Wiggins stood out in his own right. Originally from the Bronx, New York, Jewell completed a prep school year at Notre Dame Prep in Fitchburg, Massachusetts. He was known for his tough defensive play and quickly earned substantial minutes as the backup point guard. Jewell played all four seasons at Rutgers University and graduated from their prestigious school of business. He embodied the mentality of the "Y" generation or Millennials, often challenging others with his tenacity.

The final freshman was Jason McCoy from Houston, Texas. He was a long and athletic wing player standing at 6'7", known for his passionate and intense style of play. However, since the recruiting staff that brought him in was no longer part of Rutgers, Jason began questioning his decision. This behavior is common among Millennials today, as they tend to question decisions and seek to fulfill their own desires by transferring between schools.

As a result, I had to travel to Jason's hometown in Houston, Texas to re-recruit him, even though he had already signed a national letter of intent binding him to the school. This has become a regular occurrence in the profession and the world today. When things don't go the Millennials' way, they often question the decisions made by authority figures or choose to quit the situation altogether.

The returning players were led by an upperclassman named Rashad Kent, who had been named a second team All-Big East performer.

Rashad Kent

Standing at 6'7" and weighing 270 pounds, Rashad was one of the conference's top athletes and reminded me of Zion Williamson from Duke University. He excelled in rebounding and was also recognized as a first team All-Defensive player.

We also had two other seniors on the team. Mike Thompson, a scholarship red-shirt senior originally from New Zealand but a transfer from Brigham Young University, saw limited playing time but provided strong leadership for the underclassmen. The second senior, Connor Fox, was a walk-on player who consistently inspired the team throughout the season. His guidance as an upperclassman played a crucial role in the early development of the new players. Connor graduated from Rutgers with honors, and I am confident he has put his degree to good use.

Additionally, there were several promising sophomores on the team. Sean Axani stood out as a two-year starter and served as the team captain during his senior year. His exceptional leadership played a significant role in our team's journey to the championship game of the post-season NIT against the University of Michigan at Madison Square Garden. Sean graduated with honors from Rutgers University's prestigious College of Business and later leveraged his degree to excel in the business world.

Herve Lamizana was a fascinating Millennial player on our team, fluent in multiple languages, a black belt in martial arts, and possessing the most significant potential as a basketball player on the team. Hailing from the Ivory Coast in Africa, Herve completed two years of high school education at Saint Patrick's in New Jersey, where he played under the successful coach Kevin Boyle. Kevin later became the head coach at the renowned Montverde Academy in Florida.

Touted as a promising professional prospect, Herve lived up to expectations, playing in China as one of Asia's highest-paid professional basketball players. He also played a crucial role in Rutgers' NIT national championship run.

We also had two other returning upperclassmen post players, Kareem Wright and Eugene Dabney. Standing at 6'10" and weighing 285 pounds, Kareem was an imposing force inside the paint. After graduation, he went on to have a successful career with the Harlem Globetrotters. The other upperclassman, Eugene, was highly recruited from a junior college. Although he only played one season at Rutgers before transferring to an NAIA powerhouse program, he contributed significantly to the team's success. In fact, his new team won the NAIA Championship the following year.

Additionally, we had three returning walk-ons: Justin Piasecki, Sloan Baptiste, and Mitch Garrett. Each of them brought a strong work ethic and provided support to the team in their own way. Despite not being on scholarship and volunteering their time, they were just as important as any other member of the program. We respected and valued their contributions, recognizing the unique service they brought. However, like all the other players, they were Millennials, and as a coaching staff, we had to understand and adapt to their personal challenges and issues.

THE EMERGENCY ROOM SAGA CONTINUES...

I was reminded of the walk-ons in my first year at Rutgers when I saw the volunteer staff in the hospital's emergency room. They were not official employees, but they provided vital support services and comfort to the patients, just like the walk-ons did for our team. They worked with dedication and compassion, despite their age and status. Most of them were retired or elderly attendants from the Baby Boomer generation, born between 1946-64. The only thing that set them apart from the regular hospital staff was their attire.

The Baby Boomers were hailed as one of the greatest generations due to their efforts in rebuilding the nation's capital and establishing global relationships. During their generation's early years, the wealth and Gross Domestic Product (GDP) experienced steady growth, and the Baby Boomers seized every opportunity presented. The GDP, a common indicator of economic health, played a significant role in their era. These Baby Boomers, as parents, sacrificed and fought to provide their children with a life vastly different from their own, with some of those children belonging to the Millennial generation. Despite this, they still instilled a service-oriented attitude in their children, aligning with the behavior of relational development.

As the year progressed, we developed stronger connections and attachments with the players (Millennials) we inherited, as well as with the university and the people in the surrounding East Coast areas. We were dedicated to building relationships that we believed would last a lifetime.

In our inaugural season in the Big East, we achieved numerous accomplishments. We climbed five spots in the conference standings compared to the previous season, earning a post-season invitation to the NIT. Throughout the season, we defeated four nationally ranked teams. Personally, I received the honor of being named Coach of the Year by the Metropolitan Writers Association of New York. However, I must mention, I do believe this honor should've been given to the entire staff as opposed to a single coach, since we all played major roles in the team's success.

We achieved all these things despite having limited knowledge of our new associates and despite our unfamiliarity with the region. But the journey had just begun, and our group's character would be tested. The core values we established would be crucial for the survival of this early group of Millennials in our program and the university. That summer, we focused on each player's commitment to the program during the summer sessions.

Our objective was to instill in each player the program's Core Values of Character: integrity, honesty, trust, respect and loyalty. I will discuss each core value in more detail throughout the chapters to show how we helped our Millennials cope better with the pressures that society imposed on them. My ultimate goal was to create relationships based on character and mutual respect that would bridge the generational gap.

Chapter 4:

DEFIANT BEHAVIOR

"Your behavior is the mirror of your personality and character, and your attitude is it's reflection."

—**Sagar Dubey,** Indian Actor

After a relatively successful first year at Rutgers University, we found ourselves at a crossroads, contemplating the direction we wanted to pursue. At the outset of my tenure, our athletic director, Bob Mulcahy, made it clear that we should retain all the players from the previous year, considering the stressful and challenging circumstances they had endured.

Bob was an unconventional athletic director, with limited prior experience in athletic administration. His background primarily involved political leadership positions, such as

Bob Mulcahy

CEO of the New Jersey Sports and Exposition Authority, operating the Meadowlands Sports Complex in Newark. He was also the former mayor of Mendham and was appointed to be the Deputy Commissioner of the New Jersey Department of Institutes and Agencies by Governor Brandon Byrne. His strong political connections made him an asset for the State University of New Jersey.

A testament to those connections occurred during my first year at Rutgers when Bob introduced me to the then-NBA Commissioner and Rutgers graduate, David Stern. He had come to visit New Brunswick to assess the university's progress and share some encouraging words over lunch. I vividly remember his message that day. He acknowledged my achievement as the first African-American head basketball coach at Rutgers and commended the positive and exemplary things he had heard about me.

His final words resonated deeply: "Do it your way and don't let negative outside forces interfere with your integrity. Your character is what truly matters." David Stern's passing in 2020 marked the end of an era, leaving behind a legacy of character unparalleled by any other commissioner in any sport. His influence will transcend generations.

David Stern

I took both David Stern's advice and everything the players had gone through to heart, understanding the challenges the players had faced in the toxic environment and respecting Bob's request to retain them. However, I couldn't ignore the potential long-lasting effects this situation might have had on their well-being. It lingered in the back of my mind, leaving me with limited alternatives. As a result, I couldn't rule out the possibility of player elimination in the upcoming year.

This group of players was unlike any I had encountered before. Was it due to their Millennial generation or their East Coast origins? I believe their generational makeup played a more significant role.

Millennials, or Generation Y, born between the early 1980s and mid-1990s, possess unique characteristics. Researchers describe them as confident, open-minded, self-expressive, liberal, tech-savvy, and receptive to new ideas from trusted sources.

However, they can also be self-centered, lazy, entitled, narcissistic, and prone to jumping from one situation to another. As mentioned in the previous chapter, this generation doesn't see transferring between schools as an issue. In fact, the NCAA has facilitated this by creating a portal format.

The portal format allows student-athletes to submit their information for immediate transfer and eligibility at another school if they meet the NCAA's requirements. Imagine if this process had been in place during the early years of the recruiting process – it would have opened the doors to all kinds of unethical practices and maneuvers.

In today's college basketball landscape, I believe the NCAA and the basketball profession as a whole are better equipped to handle the challenges posed by transfers. The fifth-year transfer ruling has gained prominence and brought the transfer portal to the forefront of discussions. However, there's a part of me that is concerned about the potential dominance of the transfer portal, which could lead to irreversible situations.

As we looked ahead to the upcoming season, excitement buzzed through our program. We had a talented group of players, mostly underclassmen and all Millennials, who brought a fresh energy to the team. Graduation only took away two seniors, with one of them being a significant contributor on the court. We did encourage another player to transfer due to behavioral issues, but the team was mostly intact, and we only needed to bring in three support players.

Our starting five was solid, and the young players coming off the bench had gained valuable experience. Expectations were high, fueled by the promising season we had just experienced. This allowed us the luxury of focusing our energy on recruiting for the following year, looking to build upon our success.

NLI NATIONAL LETTER *of* INTENT

Year 20___ / 20___

Name of Prospective Student-Athlete

Last   First   Middle Initial

Permanent Address

City   State   Postal Code   Country

Prospective Student-Athlete's NCAA ID   **Date of Birth**

(must be registered with the NCAA Eligibility Center and on the Institutional Request List)

Submission of this NLI has been authorized by:

SIGNED

Director of Athletics (or designee)   Date Issued to Prospective Student-Athlete

For Institutional Use Only:
☐ Two-year college transfer
☐ 2-4 Qualifier ☐ 2-4 Nonqualifier
☐ Two-year college graduate   Expected graduation date _____

Sport

This is to certify my decision to enroll at _____

Name of Institution

National Letter of Intent (NLI)

The early signing period for the National Letter of Intent (NLI) fell in mid-November, just a week before the start of the season. The NLI is a binding document that commits a player to a specific institution for a defined period of time.

Two eye-opening situations during the recruiting period demonstrated this generation's unique way of thinking and behavior. I had never experienced anything like it at Kent State or any other school where I coached at the collegiate level. This group of Millennials seemed willing to compromise their own success to put themselves in the spotlight—a trait some believe is part of their generation's DNA: self-absorption and self-centeredness.

On separate occasions, we brought in two highly publicized and major recruits who later became NBA players after leaving other universities. One recruit, Josh Boone, signed with the University of Connecticut two years later and helped them win a national championship in his second year. Unfortunately, Josh had a compromising experience and was mistreated by his host player and four others during his official visit to our campus.

Ironically, Josh was already prepared to commit to us, so the visit was meant to be a formality and a confirmation of his commitment. I had warned the players beforehand, "The only way he won't commit is if you guys mess up this visit." Josh was just 17 years old at the time, young for a graduating senior, and hailed from a small school in the Maryland suburbs. As a result, other Division 1 schools hadn't fully recognized his potential at that early stage of his life. However, this negative experience led Josh, his mother, and his AAU coach to decide that he should forgo college for the time being and pursue the prep school route. It was there that he truly blossomed and caught the attention of top Division 1 universities.

Josh and his mother made their decision based on how this group of self-centered Millennials treated him. These players, focused solely on themselves and threatened by the recruit's potential, failed to consider how their actions would impact their team's future success. This was the first of many negative occurrences that surfaced throughout the year.

We were still working on building trust with each other as the early recruiting period ended with this group of Millennials. Trust was the main core value I asked from everyone in this basketball program. The Webster Dictionary defines trust as "a firm belief in the reliability, truth, ability, or strength of someone or something" and "acceptance of the truth of a statement without evidence or investigation." This simply means you are someone others can depend on because you do what you say. I wanted our relationships to be built on trust and honesty without fear of repercussions.

This led us to another situation that involved trusting each other, which showed this generational group's true colors. The last major recruit we had on campus was Aaron Grey, a 7-foot giant who later signed with the University of Pittsburg. He played in the NCAA Tournament every year he was there.

Like Josh Boone, Aaron was ready to commit to us, and the only thing that could stop him was how the players in the program interacted with him. I had talked to each team member about how important this recruit and his visit were. I also explained how they could influence his decision. Despite past experiences warranting caution, I wanted to trust them, as we were in this together, whether I liked it or not.

Trust is the cornerstone of any genuine relationship. So, I had to reveal my cards, so to speak, if I wanted to help this group of Millennials make any progress or commitment. But I should have known that getting burnt once could happen again, especially by the same people. Albert Einstein once said, "Insanity is doing the same thing over and over again and expecting different results." I should have known that this was madness!

In the final stages of Aaron's recruiting visit, an unexpected incident unfolded, completely shifting the commitment situation. We were at the campus football game, enjoying ourselves with Aaron and his family. Up until that moment, everything had been going smoothly, and Aaron had expressed his readiness to commit. All that remained was sealing the deal with his parents. However, chaos erupted in the end zone of the stadium bleachers, disrupting the atmosphere.

A member of our basketball program dashed toward us, urgently informing me, "Coach, you need to come to the end zone bleachers. Our players are involved in a fight and they need your help."

As I arrived at the scene, I witnessed three of our players engaged in a physical altercation with fraternity members while campus police struggled to restore order. Eventually, the fight was brought under control,

Rutgers Football Stadium

but I watched two of our players being led away in handcuffs, while Aaron and his parents observed the entire ordeal. In that moment, I knew our chances of securing Aaron's commitment to Rutgers University had evaporated.

When I spoke with them immediately after the unnecessary incident, I could sense the tension in their voices as they expressed their clear stance: "We do not want our son in this type of environment." Once again, the program fell victim to the behavior and antics of this particular group of Millennials, exemplifying the self-centered attitude often associated with their generation. It was all about them, regardless of who suffered as a result.

Another memorable situation occurred early in our non-conference season that year. We faced the University of North Carolina in a nationally televised game in Raleigh, North Carolina. We held the lead throughout the entire game until the last two minutes when one of our players took matters into his own hands. To protect his identity, I won't disclose his name.

With a four-point lead and just two minutes remaining, we had possession of the ball. In a baffling move, the player launched an ill-advised three-point shot well before the shot clock expired. It was a terrible miss, allowing them to secure the rebound and transition into a fastbreak, scoring on that possession. Recognizing the need to regroup, I called a timeout to address the team with a little over a minute left in the game.

In the huddle, everyone was aware of the time and score, as well as the play we intended to run when the shot clock reached a certain point. But once again, a surprising turn of events occurred within 15 seconds of that possession. The same player disregarded the plan and took another ill-advised shot, leaving the entire team and coaching staff bewildered. As you can imagine, we ended up losing the game under immense pressure.

Yet, what frustrated me even more wasn't the sequence of events that led to our defeat. It was the player's response in the locker room after the game. I found him sitting in the corner, with a towel over his head, sobbing. I approached him to offer comfort and alleviate some of his anxiety.

What happened next encapsulated the essence of this generation. I said to him, "This could have happened to anyone, so don't let it get you down. We all played a part in the meltdown." His response struck me deeply. He said, "It was my fault. I'm not crying because we lost the game; I'm crying because I let myself down and the pro scouts who were here watching me. I blew my opportunity!"

At that moment, he wasn't thinking about the team or the game we had lost. His focus was solely on himself and how he appeared to others. This self-centered attitude is prevalent among many Millennials today, making it difficult to reach them without seeing the world through their lens. It is our responsibility to address this behavior and help them improve their value structure.

Throughout the year, we dedicated ourselves to teaching and guiding this group of Millennials, emphasizing character and values. While we succeeded in helping some of them, a few were lost along the way. It led us to emphasize a primary core value: trust. This value became the focal point of our efforts that year because it was evident that these Millennials needed guidance. Each circumstance we encountered during that time served as a stark reminder of the importance of trust and the challenges we faced in instilling it within them.

THE EMERGENCY ROOM SAGA CONTINUES...

In the previous chapters, I emphasized the importance of trust among the Millennial attendants working in the emergency room. With their immense responsibilities, caring for numerous patients in a short amount of time and under stressful circumstances, they must embody the character that represents the entire hospital staff. Trust becomes a vital value within the team.

After waiting for over an hour in the lab to have my blood drawn, I approached a male nurse who was sitting at the lab entrance. Many patients were expressing their frustrations about the service and long wait times. I could see the overwhelming stress on his face, which eroded my trust in the quality of care he could provide.

When he finally called my name, I entered a room that hadn't been properly cleaned, and a syringe lay visible on the floor. It was appalling to witness such neglect in a hospital setting. I tried to engage in a conversation with the aid before he began drawing blood, but it seemed he cared more about rushing through the process than the condition of the surroundings.

He had trouble finding a vein in my arm and jabbed the needle clumsily. I felt a surge of distrust and anxiety. The next thing I knew, I had fainted on the filthy floor. It was a terrible experience, being in a stressful situation with a healthcare provider who didn't earn my trust. It made me think of players who face stressful situations and don't trust their coaches. Imagine how they would feel, having someone in charge of their wellbeing who they don't believe really care about them.

Despite a rocky start to our recruiting process in the second year, we remained determined to steer the program in the right direction—toward the next level in the Big East. At the time, the Big East consisted of 16 teams, making it one of the largest conferences in the country. The conference was divided into four quads, with the quad system designed to showcase top teams when they faced each other for television exposure. The schools included Syracuse, Georgetown, Seton Hall, Rutgers, Providence, Connecticut, Villanova, Pittsburgh, St. John's, West Virginia, Miami, Boston College, Florida State, Louisville, DePaul, and Virginia Tech. It was considered the best basketball conference in America!

Each team in a quad played all the other teams in their quad twice, along with two teams from the quad above or below them. The rest of the schedule consisted of eight other teams from the remaining two quads, played once over a two-year period until facing each team in the conference.

Our goal was to break into the top tier and advance to the next level. We were on the verge of achieving that, thanks to the success we had in our first year in the league. Being in the highly ranked Big East Conference meant facing intense competition and challenging games night after night. Moreover, playing on someone else's home court put us at a distinct disadvantage.

The season began on a positive note with early non-conference victories. However, after the unnecessary loss at North Carolina, we had to regroup and get back on track. We managed to secure a win in the next game against Temple University, led by the Hall of Famer, John Chaney, which gave us a much-needed boost to kickstart the conference season.

The Big East season proved to be extremely challenging and difficult. We were well aware of our position right from the start. The quad system was put in place to establish a hierarchy, and the coaches, teams, and officials understood their roles within it. However, I never settled for the "status quo" and consistently fought against it throughout my time in the Big East Conference.

After being eliminated from the Big East tournament, I faced some difficult decisions that went against the initial requests of my athletic director. I chose to move on from a few players who still had eligibility, including one who was a starter. It was time to fully imprint our program with the character-driven approach we sought.

This decision propelled us into one of the most successful seasons in recent history for Rutgers. The team, composed of a group of young Millennials, was ready to change the landscape and put Rutgers on the map in the Big East and the entire country.

Chapter 5:

ELECTRONIC DISTRACTIONS

"The distraction, particularly of technology, impedes the innovations process. And when you add to that the distraction of working with (others), who have a different approach to urgency and distraction, the potential for losing focus is abundant."

—David Livermore, PhD, Social Scientist

This recruiting class was truly unique – it consisted entirely of Millennials. These young athletes proved to be the driving force behind our remarkable run in that year's postseason tournament. They achieved far more than anyone anticipated, but still fell short of their full potential.

As the team underwent significant changes – with three players graduating, two others leaving the program, and new recruits joining – we were determined to create the perfect blend of talent and character. Our goal was to assemble a group of high achievers with strong values, excelling in the classroom, on the court, and in their personal conduct.

However, there was one aspect of this Millennial generation we couldn't escape: their ever-present electronic devices. This marked the dawn of the technology-obsessed generation. They referred to themselves

as the "connecteds." Tim Elmore, in *Generation iY*, notes the impact of their digital connectivity. "Because so much of their life is connected by technology, young people can fail to develop face-to-face people skills."

These young athletes often felt lost without their smartphones, constantly checking social media and texting. Elmore argues that texting "doesn't prepare this generation to interact in real relationship dilemmas." In his view, "screens are for information – not emotions," and genuine interpersonal skills are essential for success in today's society.

Every player on the team had a mobile phone and any other electronic gadget they could get their hands on. Mobile phones had taken over as their primary form of communication. The landline was becoming less relevant and useful, making the cell phone the preferred device for this generation.

As a result, contacting players on their dorm room landlines proved challenging. To address this, I implemented a rule stating that the players had to respond within fifteen minutes whenever they received a call or message from the coaching staff.

As communication technology continued to evolve, it began to permeate all generations, including the Baby Boomers. As coaches, we had to adapt and embrace these changes or risk being left behind. However, there were certain times and places where I could not allow electronic devices to take precedence in the players' lives. These included the classroom, office, meetings, practices, and the Training Table.

The Training Table was a designated area where we shared nutritious meals from Monday to Friday. It also served as a social space where I encouraged the players and coaches to interact and bond. Consequently, all electronic devices, including cell phones and headphones, had to be turned off and kept out of sight during these times. This rule initially proved challenging for both players and coaches.

The reason for this difficulty for the Millennials was that they had been allowed to use these devices around their parents and other adults without restriction. To me, this behavior was akin to wearing hats at the dinner table or other respectable places, which has also become a tolerated practice as the respect and courtesy that used to be a social standard have seemingly lost their significance.

In our program, I insisted that players and coaches alike shut down their devices and remove any headwear in certain areas to demonstrate respectful behavior. Their parents appreciated our enforcement of this rule. My hidden agenda, however, was to instill a sense of decorum and civility in our players, hoping they would pass on these behavioral values to their future children, players, or other young people they might mentor one day. We came up with a catchy phrase to reinforce this rule: "Check yourself before you come in!" It meant they had to be courteous and conscious of their settings.

By my third year at Rutgers, every player in the program was a Millennial. However, this particular incoming class displayed a maturity beyond their years. They were perfectly suited for the challenges ahead and consistently demonstrated respect and strong values in all their endeavors. Four players were added to this class and made significant contributions to

Quincy Douby

the program during their time with us.

Quincy Douby emerged as a standout player and was eventually chosen in the NBA draft lottery at the end of his junior year. He was undeniably the steal of the class. Quincy was from Washington Heights in Brooklyn, New York, and graduated from Grady High School. His coach, Jack Ringel, was a seasoned veteran in the city and a father figure to Quincy. Jack, may he rest in peace, mentored Quincy throughout junior high and high school, shaping him into the exceptional athlete he became.

Quincy was the best shooter to ever come out of Brooklyn. I'd seen some great shooters in my time, but Quincy was something special. He had a smooth, effortless stroke that could hit from anywhere on the court. The only other player I'd seen with a shot like his was Glenn Rice, who went on to win a national championship at Michigan and have a successful NBA career. Quincy still holds the Big East record for consecutive three-pointers made in a game, with eight against Syracuse.

Marquis Webb was the stability of the class. He was an all-state performer at Patterson Catholic in New Jersey, and he brought a lot of character and leadership to the team. Marquis was a four-year starter at Rutgers, and he captained the team both on and off the court.

He went on to become a Division 1 college assistant basketball coach. After his tenure there, he transitioned to head coach at Patterson East Side

High School in his home state of New Jersey. During his time there, he was awarded Coach of the Year. Due to his success, he secured a position at Morristown Beard School, where he is currently coaching.

Marquis Webb

Byron Joynes was a physical specimen. He was 6'9" and 270 pounds, and he came out of Oak Hill Academy, a powerhouse prep school in Virginia. Byron was a teammate of Carmelo Anthony on a state championship team in Baltimore, and he had the potential to be a dominating player himself.

The fourth player in the class was Eric Hazard, a 6'6" guard/forward from Long Branch, New Jersey. Eric spent his first season as a redshirt freshman, focusing on improving his physical and skill development. These four players were instrumental in our success and the revitalization of the program during our final three years at Rutgers University. They helped us turn the program around.

These millennials were a contradiction to the stereotypes that are often associated with their generation. They defied the labels of being entitled, unprepared, pessimistic slackers, who were overly reliant on their parents, as paraphrased from Chris Tuff's book, *The Millennial Whisperer.*

Tuff further debunks these myths, stating that millennials are often wrongly perceived as believing they are better at their profession than others, quick to quit when upset, and needing video games to be productive. These misconceptions did not apply to our group of millennials.

Tuff also emphasizes a fundamental truth: given the right environment, a supportive culture, and key opportunities—like what we provided at Rutgers—millennials could flourish and thrive under most circumstances. Our group of millennials possessed the character and values needed to withstand the pressures of their generation.

Regarding academics, Tuff notes that younger millennials experienced change differently than their older counterparts. They grew up with cell phones and iPods, and by the time they reached adolescence, smartphones were a staple. His book reminded me that these millennials never had to visit a library for research; they had the internet at their fingertips.

This shift in the academic landscape even took our academic coordinator, Randy Larson, by surprise. Randy supervised our study tables and was an exceptional coordinator who genuinely empathized with and cared for our student-athletes, going above and beyond in her commitment to their academic success. Ultimately, my entire staff had to adapt and learn how to work with and support the development of this generation.

Randy Larson

As Chris Tuff puts it, "these earlier millennials were thrown the entire playbook that worked during their most critical years of growth, and then was given a whole new playbook—before they had the tools to adjust and pivot." But they adapted to this situation and became leaders during their time at Rutgers.

For example, after my first year coaching at the USA training trials, I was selected to coach the junior national team the following year. This team included future NBA prospects like Carmelo Anthony, an eventual NBA All-Star and Olympic gold medalist; Chris Bosh, a member of the Miami Heat Championship teams; Andre Iguodala, part of the Golden State Warriors Championship teams; and Deron Williams, a perennial all-star for several NBA teams, among others.

We held our early practice sessions during the Junior World Championship qualifying games in Miami, Florida at the Miami Heat arena. We practiced there before traveling to Venezuela on the northern coast of South America, where the qualifying games would be held.

After our first practice, we had a team dinner at our Miami hotel. The other coaches were Ernie Kent, then head coach at the University of Oregon, and Bob McKillop of North Carolina Davidson, who coached Stephen Curry of the Golden State Warriors.

USA Junior National Team

After we had eaten, we brought all the chairs together to become more acquainted with each other. We started the chat session off by introducing ourselves with a designed format. We asked each person to stand-up to say their name, where they were from, identify their siblings, and talk about any other family members they wanted to mention.

The coaches began the session, and I went first. When I mentioned being married for over thirty years, the room fell silent. In unison, the players exclaimed, "How could you be married to the same woman for such a long time and still want to be together?" They couldn't envision themselves in a similar situation, as it wasn't part of their generational makeup. Some were raised in homes without a father figure, so being married to one woman wasn't a familiar concept.

We immediately discussed the topic, and they did not see being married to one person for thirty years as a testament of one's character, they saw it as a hinderance on their lifestyle. They couldn't accept our generation's perspective on this matter. What we also learned from them was that they desired the freedom to explore their own interests without the perceived constraints of marriage.

Nevertheless, I found leading these young men at Rutgers and on the USA Junior National Team was not much different than the previous generation I had encountered. They were all talented athletes who were eager to learn and grow. They were also all motivated to succeed, and they were willing to put in the hard work necessary to achieve their goals.

THE EMERGENCY ROOM SAGA CONTINUES...

I couldn't help but draw parallels between the millennials I encountered in the ER I mentioned in previous chapters and those I worked with on the basketball court. After waking up on the lab floor, I was helped onto a nearby gurney. A male nurse began talking to me as I regained consciousness.

Once I was alert, I noticed his attention had shifted from me to his cell phone. For the next hour, as I lay on the gurney, the young nurse was preoccupied with talking and playing games on his phone. When I asked him his age and a few other questions, he replied, "I'm 19 years old, and I only have 30 minutes left in this place. I'll be glad when my shift is over since I have more important things to do."

It was evident that his respect for his job was minimal, and it appeared he was only working for a paycheck. So, where did I stand in the pecking order with this millennial? I was clearly no match for his electronic device, which he held the entire time, nor did he prioritize his role as a caretaker for the patients in his care.

The season began with impressive victories over teams like Temple University, coached by Hall of Famer John Chaney, Penn State University, and Northwestern University of the Big Ten Conference. However, I was uncertain how the incoming freshmen and returning players would coexist in a challenging environment like New Jersey and the Big East Conference.

One thing I did know was that these freshmen were talented, extremely competitive, and embodied many positive traits. Combining these qualities with those of the returning players, I believed we had a chance to achieve great success that season.

As we entered the Big East conference season, we had established ourselves as contenders within the league standings—a position typically held by conference leaders who didn't expect lower-tier teams to break into the upper echelon.

This group of millennials faced daily challenges in multiple ways. First, in the classroom, as Rutgers prided itself on being on par with Ivy League schools in the East. With Princeton just down the road in New Jersey, Rutgers felt the pressure to emulate them.

Rutgers College

Rutgers' educational standards were high, and basketball players were required to enter through Rutgers College, the campus's most prestigious college with the highest academic qualifications. Their standards were equivalent to those of the Ivy League schools they compared themselves to.

The other colleges on campus didn't have the same standards, and we were the only sport on campus required to go through this college. I prefer not to get into a full discussion of why the standards were different, but the men's and women's basketball teams were the only programs required to do this, and both had black head coaches. The women's team at Rutgers was coached by Vivian Stringer, a Hall of Fame inductee. So, read between the lines!

Another challenge these millennials faced was on the basketball court. That season, the Big East was considered the number one Division 1 conference in the country. This was primarily because Syracuse had won the national championship the previous year, and Connecticut was considered the front runner for this year, both being Big East powerhouses.

This was undoubtedly a tough and competitive league. It had produced several All-Americans and many professional players in recent years. This message was communicated to me during my first year at Rutgers by Jim Boeheim, the head coach at Syracuse, and Jim Calhoun, the head coach at Connecticut.

They shared this insight during the USA Basketball trials: "To be competitive in this league, you need to have at least two potential pros on the court most of the time." After being in the league those first two years, I found this statement to be true, as I witnessed the presence of these potential pros on a game-by-game basis.

I felt it was time to place my trust in these young millennials, allowing them to take the next step towards prominence. Despite living in a world defined by instant gratification and the expectation of getting what they want when they want it (Simon Sinek, *Leaders Eat Last*), they were also immersed in the electronic frenzy that had become a part of their daily lives.

I believe that technology is a tool that defined this generation and many of the players in our program. But the direction where this group of millennials were headed far exceeded the value they put on the tools they used to function throughout the day. I realized that if we allowed technology to be a distraction, it would interfere with the success of our program. But if we embraced technology and used it to our advantage, it could be a powerful tool for learning and growth.

It was clear that technology is here to stay, so I knew we had to embrace and keep up with this ever-changing world that the millennials were evolving with and adapting to. Still, I agree with Bill Gates' sentiment: "Technology is just a tool. In terms of getting the kids working together and motivating them, the teacher is still the most important."

Chapter 6:

REWARDING EFFORT

"Awards are so unnecessary because I think we get so much out of our work just by doing it. The work is a reward in itself."

—**Natalie Portman**, American Actress

Media Day—the kick-off event for any sports season—is electric with anticipation and optimism. Coaches and players alike feel invincible because for the time being, everyone is on a level playing field with no team having any discernible advantages.

This event bridges the gap between the team and the media, so across the country, universities use media day as an opportunity to introduce their teams and share their insights on the upcoming season. The head

Media Day

coach and a couple of players from each school sit down with reporters, photographers, and broadcasters, following a set schedule. Some media day events are bigger than others, but they all matter. It's a chance to make a good impression, to build relationships, and to generate some hype.

Every head coach has to attend the Big East media day, which happens about a month before the college basketball season starts. Each coach has to talk about their team and their expectations for the season.

It's an event that sets the stage for media commentaries and pre-season predictions. That season, I was feeling optimistic, confident our Millennials had the tools to handle whatever challenges that lie ahead.

Throughout the conference season, we battled fiercely and competed relentlessly, remaining in contention until the very end. If not for the setback of losing three out of our last four games, with the final two defeats totaling a mere three-point difference, we would have secured a top position in the conference. I also believe that this would have earned us an automatic bid to the NCAA Tournament.

One of those losses was a heartbreaker against Virginia Tech, with a tip-in basket at the buzzer snatching our victory despite leading throughout the game. This defeat was followed by another narrow 2-point loss to Seton Hall, led by former NBA player Lewis Orr. These losses cost us our automatic bid to the NCAA Tournament. As I've often said in this profession, "You can be very close, but not close enough to receive the prize."

But after bowing out early in the first round of the Big East Tournament by Virginia Tech again in another last-second defeat, there was no prize in sight for just participating. Come in first – here's your trophy. Come in last? Here's your trophy, too. In fact, here's a trophy for everyone!" muses Simon Sinek, in *Leaders Eat Last*.

He writes, "The use and overuse of extrinsic rewards do not add up to greater inner drive." He adds, "Giving out awards is good, giving out awards to everyone who participates is not necessarily better." This resonates with my belief—even if you compete fiercely enough to be in contention for the award, there's still a chance you might finish second.

EMERGENCY ROOM SAGA CONTINUES . . .

The thought of coming in second reminds me of the trepidation I felt during the ER experience. Now, after my ordeal in the blood lab, I was transported to the basement area of the hospital, parked on a gurney in the hallway. Having been left there for over two hours, I definitely felt like an afterthought. I had been in the ER for four hours without any sign of progress, much less a "prize."

While I was lying on a gurney in the crowded hallway, two female aides who saw how uncomfortable I was, came over and tried to console me. We talked for quite some time and during our conversation they mentioned their age; they were Millennials. One of them told the other about my extended wait and said doctors should have attended to me earlier. They both emphasized the importance of showing consideration to older patients in their care under emergency circumstances. Their dedication to comforting and respecting their older patients—even though I didn't perceive myself as older—left a lasting impression. These two aides stood by me until the doctors arrived, showing politeness and the utmost respect.

It's funny how certain situations can catapult us into new understandings. These Millennials surprised me with their attitude because I had a different impression of their generation, who often receive criticism for being disconnected or self-centered. What I witnessed with these Millennials was a step forward. They had grown and matured in their profession and showed that when it comes to helping someone in need, it's not age that matters; it's care and respect, these are values of character.

We had high hopes of playing in the NCAA Tournament, but we'd missed our chance. It was a bitter pill to swallow for me and my players. We felt like we had worked hard and competed well, but we did not get

the reward we'd hoped for. We were offered a consolation prize: an invitation from the prestigious National Invitation Tournament (NIT) to play in their post-season event.

During those times, the NIT represented the second-best option for post-season play, drawing in some of the stronger teams overlooked by the NCAA Tournament. These were the teams that had narrowly missed out on the ultimate prize.

As a coaching staff, we were focused on winning three crucial games, which would secure us a place in the semi-finals of the tournament held at Madison Square Garden (MSG).

However, enthusiasm for a second-tier tournament was in short supply among some of our players, as their aspirations had been set to compete in the NCAA Tournament. I understood their feelings because I had been in a similar situation before. During my first year at Rutgers, we had a good year, but ended up playing in the NIT. We did not perform at our usual level and we bowed out early.

To avoid a repeat of that situation, I presented the team with an ultimatum. They were given the choice to either compete wholeheartedly or decline the NIT invitation. I gave each player and coach a separate ballot to vote, and I stated, "Whatever the outcome, this will be the final decision."

The vote was unanimous in favor of participation. Playing in the NIT may not have been our first choice, but we decided to make the best of it. We wouldn't just compete; we go for the national title. We knew it would not be easy, because we had to face some tough opponents who also wanted the prize. The prize was not just a trophy, but a chance to play at Madison Square Garden (MSG), the most famous arena in the world. Playing at MSG would validate our season, put us on the national television stage, and thrust us onto the national scene for the next year. After the vote, we held a practice session that turned out to be one of the season's best.

We were familiar with the first three teams we played in the tournament, and we successfully defeated each one. In the first game, we beat Temple University, led by John Chaney.

In the second round, we defeated West Virginia, coached by John Beilein, who was the Cleveland Cavaliers head coach from 2019 – 2020. After that, we faced Villanova University, coached by Jay Wright, a two-time NCAA National Champion. Advancing to the semi-finals at MSG was no small feat, as each team was well aware of our strategies and was vying for the chance to play.

We outlasted a feisty Iowa State team in the semi-final game at MSG, with Quincy Douby, a freshman, scoring a tournament high of 35 points. Rutgers made a strong showing throughout the three days in New York City, with fans filling trains traveling from New Jersey to Manhattan for each game. They also filled three quarters of the arena at Madison Square Garden for both contests.

Another interesting thing about the NIT that year was that all four coaches in the final four were African Americans. The other three coaches were Tommy Amaker from the University of Michigan, who is currently the head coach at Harvard; Ernie Kent from the University of Oregon, who I mentioned earlier; and Wayne Morgan from Iowa State, who we played against in the semi-finals.

This was the first time this had ever happened in a predominantly white-sponsored national tournament in the United States. It was truly a memorable moment, especially after our nation had just celebrated Black History Month. As of the time of this writing, this has not happened again - having this many African American head coaches at the Division 1 college basketball level participating in the final four of a major national tournament.

We played the championship game in front of a national audience, and it was the sole NCAA championship game televised that Monday night. We faced Michigan, coached by Amaker. It was a close and competitive contest, with both teams playing at a high level. But only one could receive the trophy. As Simon Sinek says, "In the real world, we get nothing for coming in second. Sometimes we don't even get anything for coming in first." Michigan pulled away in the final moments and won the prize. An old adage came to mind that night: "You don't have to lose to learn." (Waters Words of Wisdom)

This is an old proverb I've used throughout my entire adult life. What does it mean? It means that if you listen to wisdom when it's being offered to you, you might just avoid the trap that leads to unnecessary failure.

This was a message I tried to teach this young group of Millennials, but sometimes it fell on deaf ears. Quincy Douby had an outstanding game in the semi-finals, and I knew

NIT

from my prior experience in coaching and my relationship with Coach Amaker, that his team would be focused on shutting Quincy down.

I tried explaining to him what could happen if we did not prepare well for this, as well as having a counter to offset this strategy. Quincy heard what I was saying, but I don't think he truly listened. In the back of his mind, he felt he could overcome their game plan with his elite talent of shooting the basketball.

What happened? The inevitable occurred. Michigan played Quincy in a Box and 1 defense and he struggled the entire game. We'd prepared for it as a team, but Quincy's involvement was key, and if the key person involved doesn't believe in or hasn't sincerely listened to the game plan, in most cases they come up short.

This was a classic case of someone who did not listen and had to lose to learn the lesson.

But this one game did not define Quincy's success, nor our team's. Quincy was committed to being the best he could be every day. He used

Rutgers vs Michigan NIT

this as a learning experience to prepare him for the next season, and if I know Quincy, he's still using it in his life today.

That night, we felt incomplete for failing to win the final game. We gave our all as a young Millennial team but let the championship slip through our fingers. Philippians 3:14 (NIV) says, "[We] press on toward the goal to win the prize for which God has called [us]." These Millennials were not asking to be given anything, they only wanted the opportunity to achieve the prize.

While the outcome wasn't what we hoped, reaching the NIT championship game was monumental for developing our team and program. Getting to the final game showed how far our program had come under our leadership. What I've come to realize is something Chris Tuff stated in *The Millennial Whisperer*, "When managed in the right ways, the Millennials generation can unlock a whole new level of productivity." Our season was a testament to that, as we overachieved under the guidance of our coaches.

This group of Millennials expected to be rewarded for our successful season, regardless of the championship result. However, they didn't expect to come in second place - playing runner-up wouldn't achieve our goal of a national title. Still, we found rewards throughout the season in other ways, such as gaining valuable experience playing high-pressure games.

REWARDING EFFORT

Overall, it was an achievement just to make it to Madison Square Garden for the title game. These young men left it all on the court, learned from their mistakes, improved their skills, and developed their character. They showed me that they had what it takes to be champions in sports and life.

Chapter 7:

UNEXPECTED CHALLENGES

"When you face difficult times, know that challenges are not sent to destroy you. They're sent to strengthen you, focus you, and increase your faith."

—Spiritual Inspiration

What an ending to a season! We couldn't have scripted it any better, except for bringing home a national championship to the fans, alumni, and people of Rutgers in New Jersey who were more than overdue. Throughout the entire year, they supported their team with unwavering dedication, resulting in the most sellouts in school history.

But now, as the new season approached, we faced an important question: What was expected of this program after the success it had accomplished? We still had a team full of young Millennials, and we were about to lose two crucial parts of our machine. Herve Lamizana was leaving college, hoping to be drafted into the NBA. When that dream didn't materialize, he went on to have a successful career in China, becoming one of the highest-paid players in Asia. Sean Axani, the team's leader, graduated from the prestigious Rutgers College of Business and

Sean Axani

moved to Florida to pursue a business career. With their departures, our program became relatively young, lacking senior leadership and an experienced front line.

Herve and Sean had been our inside presence and replacing them would be paramount for us to compete in the Big East Conference and achieve any degree of success. We still had two young frontline players returning, Adrian Hill and Byron Joynes, who had shown promise.

Adrian, from Canton, Ohio, had played significant minutes the previous year and had been instrumental during our run through the NIT. I believed he would be an integral part of the team that season, but unfortunately, he suffered a serious knee injury during the summer and didn't play a single game.

Byron Joynes, a physical specimen standing at 6'9", was entering his sophomore season, making him still a young and inexperienced college player. However, his challenges on the high school and prep school level had prepared him for this moment, and I had faith that he would rise to the challenge.

Consequently, we had to totally rely on the incoming recruits, who had not played one single minute in the highly competitive Big East Conference. It was ranked once again as the No. 1 league in NCAA Division 1, with teams like Syracuse, Pittsburgh, Boston College—all ranked in the top ten nationally—and Connecticut, who was projected twelfth, boasting exceptional frontline players. Our young Millennials, unaware of the pressures and challenges they would face at this level of competition, arrived with confidence stemming from their AAU experiences, believing they could compete at any level and on any stage.

Herve Lamizana

Alana Stewart, a famous actress and model once said, "no matter what kind of challenges or difficulties or painful situations you go through in your life, we all have something deep within us that we can reach down and find the inner strength to get through them."

So, the incoming freshmen, naïve as they were, felt little pressure coming in. But little did they know, the expectations were high, after such a successful campaign the previous year. The only pressure they felt was the pressure they put upon themselves when they competed against each other in video games. Studies show that "the average teenage boy today spends more than thirteen hours a week playing video games." (Tim Elmore, *Generation iY*)

While some may argue that excessive gaming can be detrimental, some people swear that video games actually make kids smarter. The influence of video games on this generation remains a subject of debate, with mixed reviews from experts.

I cannot forget the time when we had our number one recruit, Darrel Watkins, along with two others making an official visit to our campus in the fall of 2004. We set up our locker room like an entertainment hub resembling a mini version of Dave & Busters, complete with various games and food stations.

One area was set up with table tennis, another area had billiards, and in a third area there were monitors to play video games. In our studio area, we had a large TV screen that covered an entire wall replaying our home game highlights.

It was a unique setup that impressed the recruits and their parents, creating a vibrant atmosphere. In the video area, I saw Adrian and Darrel, who signed with Syracuse University later that year, engrossed in a game of NBA 2K. It looked as though they had hit it off, but they played the entire time without uttering a single word to each other, communicating only through nods of approval. Witnessing this behavior made me reflect on the impact of video games on this generation.

Tim Elmore also highlights a disturbing piece of evidence presented by Dr. Leonard Sax, a physician and psychologist. In his book, *Boys Adrift: The Five Factors Driving the Growing Epidemic of Unmotivated Boys and Underachieving Young Men*, Dr. Sax points out that boys today, on average, are less intelligent and less capable of understanding and solving real-world problems compared to boys just fifteen years ago. Is this a result of video game dependency or is this one of those myths? The truth is, we don't know, as the evidence on this matter is not conclusive. We still need more research to understand how video games affect boys' thinking skills.

Returning to the team, we had signed three freshmen post players with unlimited potential. However, since they were untested and inexperienced, we had no idea how they would fare against some of the best post talent in the country, especially in the highly competitive Big East Conference.

Ollie Baily, a 6'6" forward from Farragut High School in Chicago, Illinois, had been a first-team all-state performer. This was the same high school that NBA Hall of Famer Kevin Garrett played. Danny Waterstradt, a 6'11" all-state performer from Redford Catholic Central High School in Dearborn Heights, Michigan, brought his skills to our team. Jimmie Inglis, a 6'9" and 250 lb. junior college transfer from Globe Institute in New York City and a native of St. Lucia in the Caribbean Islands, completed the young Millennial class.

These freshmen were thrust into action early in the season, as we lost Adrian Hill for the entire season, then an unexpected shoulder separation took Byron Joynes out of commission as well. We needed these young players to step up and perform on the frontline against some of the best talent in the country, especially when the conference began.

Ollie Bailey

These were the unexpected challenges that no one could predict, but they became our reality, and these young Millennials had to embrace the challenge since we had no other options. They were forced into action immediately, although we initially tried to put most of our dependency on the returning underclassmen from the previous year, who were also young and inexperienced. What I knew for sure was that the returning underclassmen possessed the character and leadership qualities that these young incoming Millennials needed. This team was easy to coach, and they competed to the best of their abilities throughout the entire year. However, at times, they were challenged beyond their capabilities and even our minor expectations.

EMERGENCY ROOM SAGA CONTINUES . . .

The challenges I faced in the emergency room mirrored the challenges the team encountered. After passing out on the lab floor, I was diagnosed by two doctors who initially suspected issues with my heart or brain. The first doctor wanted to keep me overnight for further tests, but after already spending six hours in the ER, I couldn't wait until the next day for answers. I demanded immediate answers and underwent a stress test and a CT scan. However, it became clear following these procedures that the doctor had no idea what was going on with me and the challenges she had to overcome to address my situation that day.

Our early non-conference games proved challenging, especially on the road. The 2004-05 season's schedule was particularly tough for our young Millennials. Unexpected personnel losses only compounded the difficulties. Yet, despite these setbacks, we managed to secure victories against strong teams like St. Mary's of California, Rhode Island, Charlotte, and Kansas State on their home courts. These early challenges tested our young players and fostered their growth.

Even with these challenges, our Millennials believed in their strong sense of connection and belonging. They faced many of the same obstacles and felt truly connected, embodying the idea that they "belong to each other" due to shared experiences and collective challenges, as underscored by Tim Elmore in *Generation iY*.

We struggled at the beginning with Big Ten Conference teams like Penn State and University of Wisconsin, who were nationally ranked, as well as road games at Princeton and Air Force. But on a surprising note, we defeated some very strong teams, such as, St. Mary's of California, who was ranked in the Top 25, Rhode Island, Charlotte, and Kansas State, which was on K-State's home court. Therefore, these young Millennials were baptized very early in the pre-season and came away all the better for it.

When the conference season began, we knew we had to elevate our level of play, regardless of our youthfulness. Every team in the Big East would come after us relentlessly. Our young front line struggled against the experienced and highly talented post players in the conference, who dominated us in every aspect of the game. We relied on our three-guard tandem to keep us competitive, hoping it would give us a chance to stay in games.

One thing was evident - our home court proved to be a competitive advantage during league play, and we were in contention in most games until the final minutes. If we had been able to close out some of the close games we lost, our conference record would have been considerably better.

As the conference season came to a close, we felt a sense of relief and took a moment to catch our breath before the Big East Tournament. The tournament was a grand event in New York City, sold out and bustling with excitement. The tournament was sold out and scalpers were at the top of their game. A pair of first-round tickets were selling for $2,000 per game. People were fighting over the limited amount left.

Madison Square Garden, despite its age, remained the most electric venue to play a tournament game in college basketball. Media presence was overwhelming, with cameras flashing at every spectacular play. This was the stage I had envisioned when I joined the Big East.

Our game was not until the evening session, giving me time to scout the first two contests earlier in the day. If we could secure a victory in our first game, our team and coaches would stay to watch at least the first half of the final game that evening, as the winner of that matchup would be our next opponent the following night.

I had committed to making the most of my time at the tournament, planning to stay for the entire day. I relished every minute, believing that each team had a fair shot at success in a conference tournament, as they all started with a clean slate. This was the beauty of holding tournaments at neutral sites.

We entered the tournament with an underdog mentality, ready to take on any challenger that stood in our way. As Roger Crawford, a NCAA Division 1 tennis player who overcame a severe disability to become a certified tennis professional, once said, "Being challenged in life is inevitable, being defeated is optional." Embracing this mindset, we were determined to leave our mark on the tournament.

Our first game in the tournament was against Notre Dame, a team we had already played tough against on their home court. Notre Dame was coached by Mike Brey, a disciple of Mike Krzyzewski of Duke, a part of his outstanding coaching tree.

It was a neutral court, and we believed we had a great chance to upset them. We outplayed them throughout the game, and our post players unexpectedly showed dominance that night. The victory filled us with joy, knowing that all the hard work and nurturing we had invested in these young Millennials had paid off. We had become accustomed to performing well in Madison Square Garden, under the bright lights and on the grand stage.

Madison Square Garden

Our next challenge was Syracuse, one of the top-seeded teams in the tournament. If we could prevail, we would reach the semi-finals and have a chance to play in the NCAA Tournament, something no Rutgers team had ever achieved in the Big East Conference.

We played with determination and competed throughout the game, but Syracuse's post play overwhelmed us. While our guard play kept us in the game during the first half, their interior dominance took control in the second half. Nevertheless, we left the tournament feeling that these young competitors had arrived in the Big East.

These young Millennials had shown me that despite being counted out due to the unexpected challenges throughout the season, they had the resilience to prevail even when their backs were against the wall. As author Steven Goodier once said, "Those who overcome great challenges will be changed, often in unexpected ways." I believed that these unexpected changes were ultimately for the best, molding these youthful Millennials into stronger individuals.

Chapter 8:

FEARFUL ANXIETY

"Anxiety is a thin stream of fear trickling through the mind. If encouraged, it cuts a channel into which all other thoughts are drained."

—**Somers Roche,** American Author

Every generation experiences fears that can surface and bring about great anxiety, and the Millennial generation is no exception. According to an article by Power of Positivity titled, *11 Behaviors that Reveal Someone Is Hiding Their Anxiety,* some Millennials feel that living with anxiety is like being followed by a voice that knows all their insecurities and uses them against them. It becomes the loudest voice, drowning out all other thoughts.

As a baby boomer in this profession, I have experienced my fair share of anxiety over the years. At times, it has taken me to dark places from which it has been difficult to return. I believe there have been other coaches who, faced with similar challenges, did not find their way back and chose to leave the sport.

I remember a conversation I had years ago with Gary Williams, a Hall of Fame recipient and a National Championship coach at the University of Maryland. He shared the anxiety he had faced with this generation and the influence of AAU Organizations on college basketball. Coach Williams expressed how he had lost interest and lacked the energy to continue the fight. It was disheartening to see a great competitor leave the sport for all the wrong reasons.

As the end-of-year banquet approached, I could feel the tension in the air the moment we entered the room. My wife, too, sensed the unease,

Gary Williams

discomfort evident on her face as she glanced at the table where she would be seated among dignitaries. Meanwhile, I would be seated on the stage, away from her for most of the evening.

I immediately moved around the room, eager to greet parents, guests, and friends. However, when I next saw my wife, I noticed a hint of sadness in her expression. Concerned, I asked her, "Is there a problem?" She responded with a pained look, saying, "I don't want to sit at that table with all those pretentious people." Her words struck a chord within me, and I could feel her pain and discomfort seeping into my own spirit.

I was already feeling some anxiety from the meeting I had earlier in the week with two board of trustee members and my athletic director, Bob Mulcahy. They were the ones seated at that table, the same individuals I had met with to discuss the past season and the future direction of the program. The meeting quickly escalated into a heated exchange, and I was taken aback by how they treated my athletic director. It bordered on disrespect.

We ended the meeting in a stalemate, and I left the room feeling disappointed. While I knew I had nothing to worry about thanks to the new contract I had signed at the end of the previous year, I couldn't shake off the discomfort caused by the direction of the conversation and the choice of words used. It left me with a lingering sense that there was no trust between the two parties.

Trust, as I mentioned in Chapter 3, is one of the core values of character. Without trust, there can be no genuine confidence or belief in your leadership. There's a quote I heard years ago that still resonates deeply with me: "Whether it's friendship or a relationship, all bonds are built on trust. Without it, you have nothing."

Observing my wife's spirit and the sadness she displayed at the back of the room, I was viscerally reminded of the unease I had experienced during the meeting. Sensing that something was amiss with the direction of the evening, I turned to her and said, "I want you to go and sit at the table with the player's parents."

This disruptive feeling continued to fester in my spirit throughout the evening, eventually casting a shadow of depression over my mood. However, something miraculous happened at the end of my speech that helped me to realize that God is real and in control.

As I took the stage to address the attendees, my disgruntlement overwhelmed me, leading me to direct my frustrations at the administrators present at the banquet. The message I delivered was so embarrassing that my athletic director shielded his face with his hands. In that moment, I had reached my breaking point, and the thought of uttering the words of resignation to the audience was on the tip of my tongue.

But something miraculous happened. The words just would not come out of my mouth. My lips were shut, as though my face was paralyzed. I came to realize it was a supernatural experience, a sign from God that it was not yet time for me to quit. What I believe He was saying to me was, "You wanted this position at Rutgers, so you have to see it through."

I concluded my message and walked off the stage without saying anything meaningful afterwards. Everyone was stunned and wondering what was going on, but I knew God was in complete control of the entire narrative, and He would decide the time of my exodus.

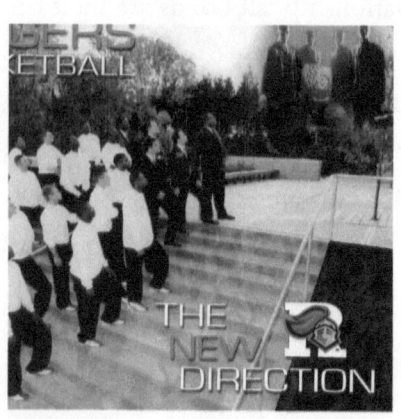

Did I have any fears about my future at Rutgers? Thoughts about what lie ahead did cross my mind, but I refused to let them hinder our objectives for the upcoming season. I had to have trust in my staff and players, so we could advance the program to a higher level, regardless of how people on the outside looking in felt. We had already outlined our goals and objectives in our *Vision Plan*, a strategy I had developed to guide the program's future over a specific timeframe, and it would be up to us to carry it out.

A vision is not merely a dream; it is the ability to think about and plan the future with imagination and wisdom. As the Bible advises, "Write down this vision; clearly inscribe it on tablets so one may easily read it. For the vision is yet for the appointed time." (Habakkuk 2:2-3, HCSB)

I believe God has given me this prophetic gift of vision throughout my adult life, even though it may not be listed among the spiritual gifts mentioned in 1 Corinthians 12:8-10. Some might mistakenly view it as the gift of prophecy or revelation, but it is truly a gift from God.

There was something else remarkable I noticed within the Millennial generation. The invincibility they often attempted to project was not true invincibility at all. I saw it as a way for them to mask the fears that are deeply ingrained in their DNA. A survey conducted by The American College Health Association in 2007 revealed that 94% of college students, including athletes, reported feeling overwhelmed by their lifestyles. Shockingly, around 44% admitted to feeling such intense depression that it hindered their ability to function, and nearly 10% had even contemplated suicide. These statistics were taken from a sample of Millennials within this generation.

Anxiety of this magnitude can stem from both internal and external sources. However, Tim Elmore notes that many of these young individuals grew up with parents who placed immense pressure on them to perform. Given these circumstances, it is not surprising that Millennials often experience self-imposed anxiety due to the undue pressures forced upon them.

Entering my final year at Rutgers, I was filled with optimism. We had recruited four exceptional individuals who represented a group of high-achieving Millennials. Three of them hailed from New Jersey, and they were among the best the state had to offer. Among them was the steal of the class J.R. Inman, a 6'9" forward from Pomona, New Jersey, who ranked in the top 100 nationally and was an all-state performer. Anthony Farmer, a first-team all-state point guard from St. Augustine Prep in Richland, New Jersey, was another standout. St. Augustine Prep was

JR Inman

renowned as one of the state's top programs. We also welcomed Jeron Griffin, an all-state forward from Manchester High School in Manchester, New Jersey.

Anthony and Jeron played on one of the top AAU programs in the state with Andrew Bynum, and they won the AAU National Championship that summer. Andrew was one of the top post players in the country. He decided to forgo his college eligibility and entered the NBA draft. We tried to bring all three of them in that class, but Bynum ended up selected as lottery pick for the Los Angeles Lakers. He later became a successful NBA player.

The final recruit we brought in was Zack Gibson, a promising 6'10"

Anthony Farmer

all-state post player from Grand Blanc, Michigan. All four of these Millennials made substantial contributions to the team and were instrumental in the remarkable turnaround from the previous season. As the non-conference season began, we experienced early success, winning six of our first seven games. Notable victories included defeating Kent State, a preseason conference favorite in the MAC, and Temple, a member of the Atlantic 10 Conference. We even triumphed over St. Mary's of California, a ranked team on their home court. These Millennials propelled us to achieve ten wins in the non-conference season, the highest total for a Rutgers team during that era.

Jeron Griffin

Once the Big East Conference commenced, we had high hopes of competing with the top teams in the league. The Big East was still considered one of the top conferences in the country. Regardless of the opponent, every game within the conference was highly competitive, often coming down to the wire.

This season was no different from the previous years, the Big East had at least five teams ranked in the top twenty polls. Consequently, we had numerous opportunities to defeat ranked opponents during conference play, without needing to venture outside the league to boost our strength of schedule, which was a key factor to the NCAA selection committee for the NCAA Tournament.

Andrew Bynum

Did anxiety accompany me as we entered Big East Conference play? Absolutely. The first four conference games served as a stark reminder of why I felt that anxiety. We started with a closely contested victory against our archrival Seton Hall on our home court, followed by an overtime loss to Villanova, ranked No. 3 in the country.

Our next challenge took us on the road to face DePaul University, a newly added member of the league. DePaul's introduction to the Big East proved to be an eye-opener as we handed them a tough defeat on their home court, with them losing seven of their first eight conference games.

And then, in the fourth game of conference play, we narrowly lost to No. 9-ranked Pittsburg. This was just the beginning of conference play in the toughest conference in NCAA Division 1 basketball, which explains the source of my anxiety.

Towards the end of conference play, something extraordinary was scheduled to take place, something that would forever alter the course of my career and life. I was to be inducted into the Varsity "K" Athletic Hall of Fame at Kent State University in February 2006—a moment any coach, in any profession, would cherish as a recognition of their life and legacy.

Hall of Fame Plaque

Naturally, I was ecstatic to be selected as a recipient of this esteemed honor. However, little did I know that the events that transpired over that fateful weekend in February 2006 would have far-reaching consequences, affecting not only me personally but also my career and the Rutgers basketball program. The date of the award ceremony was set for February 11, 2006, a Saturday evening in Kent, Ohio.

Before accepting the invitation, I checked my schedule to ensure it was feasible. At the time, the only game on the schedule was set for Monday, February 14th, against Marquette University in Piscataway, New Jersey, our hometown. Since there was no game scheduled on the Hall of Fame date, my wife and I were open to attending the ceremony.

I first informed my athletic director, Bob, about the invitation and sought his approval. He expressed his happiness for my induction but emphasized the importance of setting up everything for my departure, including arranging for the practice I would miss on Saturday, and making sure I was back to coach the game. His concern for my prompt return seemed to outweigh other considerations.

I assured him that I would do everything in my power to attend the ceremony and be back in time for practice on Sunday, ensuring the team was prepared for the game on Monday. With his agreement, we left on good terms and in high spirits. As for any pressure or anxiety about leaving the team to attend the ceremony, I felt none at all. I proceeded to have a discussion with my staff, organizing the Saturday practice for which they would be responsible. Thus, everything appeared to be in order on the home front.

The time had come for me to travel back to the place where it all started, where I received my first head coaching position—Kent State University. It was the program we built up from the bottom, accomplishing great feats along the way. This was my moment to be enshrined in Kent State's history. I only wished that the coaches who were part of our success could also be honored as inductees alongside me.

However, nobody could have predicted what would happen during the ceremony. The event proceeded as expected, and my wife and I enjoyed ourselves thoroughly. I was inducted in the Kent State Hall of

Coach & Mrs. Waters

Fame and I received a bust to commemorate this very special moment.

But outside the facility, a disturbing development was unfolding. Northeast Ohio was hit by one of the most disastrous snowstorms in its history. The magnitude of the storm rendered travel throughout the region impossible for two days. My wife and I found ourselves stuck in Kent, Ohio, unable to leave the area. The storm raged on relentlessly for 48 hours, finally subsiding late on Monday night.

EMERGENCY ROOM SAGA CONTINUES . . .

The situation was a mirror image of the storm of anxiety I endured in the emergency room. There I was, lying on the gurney in the dimly lit basement area, waiting for the doctor to decide whether I needed a brain CT scan.

The minutes ticked away, stretching into hours, then out of the blue, another doctor approached me and dropped a bombshell, saying, "You might not need a CT scan after all," heightening my anxiety even more.

The doctor explained, "I have an inkling of what's going on, but we'll need to run a few more tests to be sure."

"Will these tests help figure out the problem? And can we do them today, so I can get out of here later in the evening?" I asked hastily. The doctor seemed confident that

it could be done, but I had to place my trust in their
expertise and judgment.

This situation made me think of the biblical proverb:
"Trust in the Lord with all your heart, and lean not on your
own understanding; in all your ways acknowledge Him, and He
will direct your paths." (Proverbs 3: 5-6, NIV) Trust, you see,
holds the power to conquer fear and anxiety when you place
it in someone or something you can rely on.

Chapter 9:

GENERATIONAL DESTINATION

"In this respect, early youth is exactly like old age; it is a time of waiting for a big trip to an unknown destination. The chief difference is that youth [Millennials] wait for the morning limited, and age waits for the night train."

—**Bruce Catton,** American Historian & Author

As I accepted the unimaginable circumstances we found ourselves in, my first order of business was to call my athletic director early Sunday morning and inform him of the situation. I reassured him that I was doing everything within my power to return. I quickly faxed my staff the practice plan I had prepared earlier that morning for the Sunday evening practice, knowing I wouldn't make it back in time.

On Monday morning, I sent the staff a copy of the shoot-around workout for the afternoon. Shoot-around workouts are light practices; they shouldn't last more than an hour. They serve to review opponent plays and sets and give players some extra shooting time before the actual game. Throughout the day, I maintained constant communication with the entire staff to ensure they were fully prepared.

Right before the game, our staff meticulously discussed every detail and went over the complete game plan, leaving no room for doubt. During the game, I stayed in constant contact with at least one staff member, providing them with valuable information. They executed the game plan flawlessly, leading us to a victory over Marquette University. Associate head coach Fred Hill took the lead position and did an outstanding job.

Little did I know that Fred's coaching skills were being evaluated throughout the game as he auditioned for the head coaching position. I

Fred Hill

had only brought Fred on board that summer, making this our first year working together. While I can't say for certain that a plan was in motion, the way things unfolded certainly made one wonder. Fred, being from New Jersey and having prior experience in the Big East through his time at Seton Hall and Villanova, was a perfect fit for our program.

Once the storm subsided, my wife and I caught the earliest flight out on Tuesday morning. Upon my arrival on campus, I was bombarded by the media. They had been waiting at my office, and their relentless questions caught me off guard. They bewildered me, repeatedly asking, "Why did you leave your team without Bob's permission? Do you even care about the success of your program? Did you make every effort to get back?" I believed these questions had already been answered in previous conversations with Bob.

As I began answering the questions, I sensed an apparent disconnect between my athletic director and me. It seemed as though he didn't have my back and didn't accept or respect what I had to say about the situation. Instead of this being a moment of celebration for our program and me, it felt like a death sentence. Most other programs would have celebrated their coach's induction into a Hall of Fame, with the media showering praise. But not at Rutgers.

Being a Midwesterner in an eastern environment, I couldn't help but feel that Rutgers had never truly embraced me. At that moment, I knew it was time for me to make changes in my life, perhaps even change my destination.

THE EMERGENCY ROOM SAGA CONTINUED...

When it came to destination, my thoughts turned to the experience I had in the hospital. The only destination I was concerned about during the emergency room saga was getting home as soon as possible and putting an end to that prolonged nightmare. I was still lying on a gurney in the hospital basement because there weren't any available rooms in that area. If I were to be admitted, they would need to move me elsewhere. However, I didn't expect to be admitted.

Then, a second doctor approached with a Millennial attendant who seemed disinterested in my situation. They moved me to a room where the attendant performed a few isolated tests to rule out any heart or brain abnormalities. The testing took just over an hour. The doctor explained that the loss of blood I experienced during the night, combined with waking up in the morning and the subsequent blood drawing, caused an imbalance in my system, leading to fainting. She assured me that she knew exactly where the problem was coming from, but that revelation would have to wait until the next chapter. It's worth noting that she was not a Millennial herself.

A change in destination would have to wait since we still had five remaining regular-season games and the Big East Tournament. The pressure mounted as the week progressed, preparing for our next opponent, St. John's University. This game held significance due to the recent snowstorm fiasco and St. John's lower position in the league standings. I didn't want these young Millennials to be burdened by my personal issues.

The game was intense, and each of our players appeared on edge. It went down to the wire, and St. John's sealed a victory with a shot at the buzzer. After the game, Bob came to my office, attempting to console me on the loss, but my mind was elsewhere. Anxiety began to overwhelm me, and I left the office in despair. I didn't even stay for our usual staff meeting after the game. I needed to go home and talk to my wife. As soon as I arrived, I told her, "Right now, I'm incredibly unhappy and I want to resign." The loss in that game only intensified my desire to leave Rutgers. My wife shared my discontent, but she urged me not to make any hasty decisions without discussing it with the Lord.

The following morning, I called my lawyer, Dennis Coleman, from my office and informed him of my decision to resign. He was shocked but could sense the depth of my pain. His advice was, "Finish out the season.

You'll be performing for your next job since you're not ready to stop coaching."

Dennis worked at a respected law firm called Ropes and Gray in Connecticut. He held high regard within the basketball profession, having previously served as counsel for the NBA Players Association. Presently, he serves as lead counsel for the National Association of Basketball Coaches (NABC) in the NCAA.

Dennis Coleman

Dennis and l had been together since the moment I took the position at Rutgers.

Following that conversation, I held a brief meeting with my staff to inform them of my decision and then we prayed together. I knew my decision would impact them, so it was my responsibility to keep them informed about everything that was happening.

Next, I called Bob and asked him to come to my office to discuss my resignation. He tried to talk me out of it, but deep down, we both knew that Rutgers was not the right fit for me, regardless of the success we had achieved a year ago. I genuinely appreciated Bob's understanding during that moment, and he sympathized with my overall situation, even to the point that Rutgers ultimately honored the remaining three years on my contract.

Once I made the decision, a sense of peace washed over me that I hadn't felt in over a year. It was as if a burden had been lifted, and I was finally free. I coached the remaining four regular-season conference games with a newfound freedom I hadn't experienced since our NIT run two years prior. This helped me realize—in the words of former President Bill Clinton—"character is a journey, not a destination."

These young Millennials won three out of the four games, fighting fiercely until the end. We came close to victory against Georgetown, ranked 23rd in the country, but fell just short. Our last regular-season game was against St. John's, the team where all the discomfort had started. After defeating them convincingly, I had a unique encounter that changed some of my opinions about the Millennial Generation.

In the locker room for post-game comments, there was a knock on the door. Our manager answered, and he rushed over to inform me, "There's someone at the door who really needs to talk to you, coach. They said it's very important." I approached the door, and to my surprise, Cedric Jackson's father and high school coach, Herman Johnson Jr., stood there. Cedric was the starting point guard for St. John's, a player we had recruited two years ago but ultimately signed Quincy Douby instead. Cedric had just played well against us in the game.

I wondered why they were at our locker room door. My initial thought was that they had come to congratulate us on the victory, which would have been a respectful gesture. However, it turned out they had come to inform me that Cedric wanted to transfer and join whichever

program I was headed to next. Now, that was significant! I advised them that we should discuss this later if Cedric was released from St. John's and I had a new coaching position.

I felt flattered, but according to

Cedric Jackson

NCAA regulations, I couldn't recruit Cedric unless he was released from his contract with St. John's. It was a typical Millennial move, wanting to transfer when things weren't going their way. However, in Cedric's case, things were actually going well for him at St. John's. Yet, he still desired to transfer, prioritizing a program that honored God and instilled character values, as he and his parents were deeply spiritual individuals. They were willing to sacrifice accolades to achieve this objective. Their response was contrary to my usual experience with Millennial parents, who often gravitated towards prestige and recognition.

It was around this time that I began to enjoy coaching again, particularly with these young Millennials. They understood the importance of the game, and I respected their commitment to our coaching staff. Respect, the fourth core value of character that I mentioned earlier in the book, was evident throughout this chapter. It involves a deep admiration for someone or something, stemming from their abilities, qualities, or achievements.

We entered the Big East Tournament with a sense of confidence in our chances of success. The tournament's location at Madison Square Garden added an extra incentive to perform at the highest level, as we had demonstrated that level of play numerous times before in that arena.

Our first matchup in the tournament was against Seton Hall, a team we sought revenge against after a loss on their home court earlier in the regular season. From the start, we dominated the game and never looked back. This victory set us up for a chance to upset Villanova University, the No. 3 ranked team in the country. We competed strongly in the first half, but their depth and experience proved too much for our young Millennials. Villanova ended our potential run in the Big East Tournament. Interestingly, they were later upset by Pittsburg in the tournament semi-finals and went on to advance to the Elite Eight in the NCAA Tournament. Our loss to a formidable team like Villanova didn't leave us feeling dejected or like failures.

A few days later, we received an invitation to the NIT (National Invitation Tournament) and successfully defeated Penn State of the Big Ten on their home court in the first round. Our next opponent was St. Joe's of the Atlantic 10, and unfortunately, we lost a close game, ending our season on their home court. Overall, we finished the season on a positive note, regaining the respect we deserved after enduring such a tumultuous year.

With the season over, it was time for me to determine my next destination. I reached out to my lawyer, Dennis Coleman, to inquire if there had been any calls regarding potential head coaching positions. He informed me that three schools had expressed interest in my services, and all three were excellent options.

One of the schools was a Power 5 program in NCAA Division 1, while the other two were Division 1 Mid-Major programs. Power 5 programs are in conferences with high-major football programs and lucrative television contracts. Mid-Major programs are a level below the Power 5 conferences and do not have the same financial resources. However, all three schools offered a quality education and highly competitive sports programs. Money and program size were tempting factors, but Dennis provided valuable advice. He urged me not to get caught up in status or financial gain but to focus on personal happiness and finding peace within the sport I loved.

His words made me truly ponder my future in basketball. I realized he had my best interests at heart. Dennis emphasized that size and money were not the most critical factors, but rather my peace of mind held the utmost importance.

At that moment, I decided I needed to be with a school that genuinely cared about me and had my back, something I felt was lacking at my previous institution. As Millennial Aubrey "Drake" Graham once said, "Sometimes it's the journey that teaches you a lot about your destination."

One school that had shown great interest in my services was Cleveland State University in Cleveland, Ohio. I was familiar with the area due to my time spent in Kent, where it all began. Kent State and Cleveland State were just 45 miles apart from each other. Choosing Cleveland as our base for recruiting made sense, as it provided ideal connections in the greater Cleveland area. As I mentioned earlier, recruiting is the lifeblood of any successful basketball program. Additionally, returning to northeast Ohio, where I would be embraced, felt like an ideal destination—a Generational Destination.

Wolstein Center

Chapter 10:

MILLENNIAL ALLEGIANCE

"Every principle that wants to command strong allegiance must make a moral case. Men want to feel that what they are doing is useful, but they want also, and mainly, to feel that it is right."

—**Henry Wallace,** American Politician

As phone calls from friends and coaches started pouring in, encouraging me to return home, one coach even remarked in the media that "Rutgers didn't even realize what they had; Waters is to coaching what the Dawg Pound is to the Cleveland Browns."

The Dawg Pound

Just three months prior, I had returned to this area to be enshrined in the Kent State Hall of Fame. I was also five years removed from having the best basketball program in Northeast Ohio. My name had resurfaced in recruiting circles throughout the state of Ohio. So, why wouldn't I want to go back to Cleveland, Ohio?

But I needed to be thorough and make an informed decision. Both of the other schools were great options, but for entirely different reasons. I had to weigh their strengths against the compelling aspects that the Cleveland area and Cleveland State had to offer.

One factor that made returning to Cleveland even more appealing was that my wife and I had grown up in big cities. Returning to Cleveland meant coming from a big city in the New Jersey area, which had many similarities. We had also grown accustomed to the advantages of big city life, such as fine dining, playhouse districts, and professional entertainment—all of which Cleveland had to offer. The other two schools were located in smaller cities, making their programs the biggest shows in town. That was another aspect to consider in my decision-making process.

Lee Reed

However, the primary reason I ultimately chose to bring my talents to Cleveland, Ohio was the people at Cleveland State and my allegiance to Northeast Ohio. I had personal connections with both the athletic director, Lee Reed, and the president, Michael Schwartz, from my time prior to Rutgers University. Lee, a former basketball player himself, understood the challenges coaches faced and was an outstanding leader. He valued servicing and empowering his staff, something the Millennial generation craved in their working environment. In *The Millennial*

Whisperer, Chris Tuff states that Millennials emphasize the importance of a program's culture and responsiveness to their needs.

The president at Cleveland State was Michael Schwartz, and he was not only an incredible leader but also an exceptional human being. I had been introduced to him during his tenure as the president at Kent State, two years before I became their coach. Our friendship grew stronger over time, as my wife worked as the director of human resources at Kent State, alongside his wife, Joanne Schwartz, the Dean of the School of Education. Once again, it became clear that personal connections played a significant role. Who you know definitely matters!

Michael Schwartz

Now, why was Cleveland State so interested in me? First, they needed someone who understood the landscape of Northeast Ohio. Recruiting in Cleveland could be challenging, similar to New York City and New Jersey, if you didn't have connections to the city. Coaches in Cleveland tended to alienate those they perceived as outsiders. I checked that box.

Second, they were seeking a coach familiar with NCAA Division 1 Mid-Major basketball. The previous coach had come from a Power 5 school and underestimated the challenges of operating a Mid-Major program and recruiting at that level with fewer resources. I checked that box as well.

Lastly, Cleveland State was looking for a proven winner, someone who had experienced success at the NCAA Mid-Major level. With teams like

Butler and Wright State in the Horizon League, known for their consistent NCAA Tournament appearances, it was crucial to bring in someone with a track record of success. I certainly checked that box.

Everything seemed to align perfectly in Cleveland, making it an ideal destination for me. However, I couldn't ignore the loyalty and bond I had with each player at Rutgers, a sentiment that was reciprocated by each of them. Despite being Millennials, known for their questionable loyalty, they had turned down offers from other universities to play for me. So, my departure would be difficult for them to handle, and they might perceive it as a disloyal act. In fact, when I resigned without informing them, they did feel that I was being disloyal to the commitment we had made to one another.

Loyalty, the fifth core value of character mentioned in the beginning of this book, is defined as a strong feeling of support or allegiance. Simon Sinek, in his book *Leaders Eat Last,* asks the question, "How can we (Millennials) ever feel committed to the teams we have if the leaders of our programs aren't committed to us?" (Paraphrased). For Millennials to feel committed to a team, the leaders of the program must show commitment to them.

This was the second time I had struggled with leaving behind players I was committed to, players who had a bright future. But such is life in NCAA Division 1 College basketball. Two weeks later, I traveled to Cleveland, Ohio to accept the head coaching position at Cleveland State University. After formally accepting the contract, a press conference was immediately held in the Wolstein Center, the home of the Cleveland State Vikings' men's and women's basketball teams.

Over fifty people attended the press conference, including several media outlets. Northeast Ohio was welcoming back one of their own.

What stood out was that a quarter of the attendees were Ohio High School coaches, excited to have me back in Northeast Ohio.

The Greater Cleveland area has become known for welcoming back its own, as seen in the return of LeBron James after his stint in Miami, Florida. When he decided to come back to Cleveland, he was accepted with open arms. It was consistent with how they responded to me.

Before I could settle at Cleveland State, there were several things I needed to take care of. First, my wife and I had to find a house and neighborhood where we felt comfortable. We had specific criteria in mind. Personally, I wanted to be in close proximity to the university and the local airport since I would be traveling frequently for recruiting and business commitments in the east.

Larry DeSimpelare

Secondly, I wanted a home that was accessible for my players, a player-friendly home. Lastly, we preferred a newly built house as I wouldn't be around often enough to handle ongoing maintenance. We settled on a home in West Lake, Ohio, just 15 minutes from the airport and no more than 25 minutes from the university. We loved the neighborhood, and it met all our criteria.

Finalizing a coaching staff that would fit the environment we were about to embrace was my next responsibility. I brought one coach with me, Larry DeSimpelare, from my previous staff at Rutgers. Larry had been with me since Eastern Michigan, and we had worked together for five years at Kent State. I had learned many lessons from my experience at Rutgers that I didn't want to repeat at Cleveland State.

Recruiting was the key to success in college basketball, so hiring the right coaches was a major priority. I had learned from experience that at least two coaches out of a five-man coaching staff needed to have ties to the city and/or Northeast Ohio.

I had been burned at Rutgers when I took my entire staff from Kent State with me. Not having a single coach from New Jersey or New York on the road for recruiting was a mistake. I mentioned this issue in a previous chapter.

But on to the point, one of the coaches I interviewed at Rutgers was Dan Hurley, but I decided to keep my staff intact out of loyalty to them. Dan went on to become the head coach at Saint Benedicts Prep in New Jersey, and we didn't get a single player from him until I hired Fred Hill— a New Jersey native—the year I resigned.

Dan also coached JR Smith, an NBA Champion with LeBron James of the Cleveland Cavaliers. JR played during the years I was coaching in Cleveland. Hurley later became the head coach at Rhode Island University and is presently the head coach at the University of Connecticut, where he's won two national championships.

To finalize my point, Dan's father, Bob Hurley was the head coach at St. Anthony's High School during the time I coached at Rutgers. St. Anthony's was the number one program in New Jersey, and his father was a New Jersey legend. He often had some of the top players in the country, and we did not get one of them. So, I was committed to not making that same mistake ever again. This is why recruiting is the life blood of college basketball.

To avoid any similar mistakes, I made sure to hire coaches with Cleveland and Ohio ties. Jermaine Kimbrough, an All-State performer from Shaker Heights High School in Cleveland, and Jayson Gee from the Dayton/Springfield area were the coaches I chose. Jayson, a mentee of mine, was someone I had considered bringing on board at Rutgers, but I didn't want him to get caught up in that environment at the time.

The plan was for Jermaine to cover Northeast Ohio and for Jayson to handle the Southeast portion of Ohio. With these two coaches, we would span most of the Buckeye State, which was our primary area for recruiting. As I mentioned earlier, when I accepted the job at Rutgers, having a home base no more than a 50-mile radius from your campus and having your state under your control were key to recruiting success.

CSU Staff Photo

We also had neighboring Michigan under our command, as it was a fertile state for recruiting, particularly in Detroit. Both Larry and I had significant connections in that state. So, I felt that we had a major part of the Midwest blanketed and under our jurisdiction.

I failed to mention one other coach, Bill Buck, who was from the Cleveland area and held the position of Director of Basketball Operations. Bill was a graduate of Cleveland State and had worked as a Graduate Assistant during that time. This staff was designed to propel Cleveland

State forward in the Horizon League and achieve success on the national stage.

The final step before settling in Cleveland was to meet with our new players, who were now part of our family. The Cleveland State Basketball program only had two scholarships available after bringing in three redshirt transfers to strengthen our roster for the next two years.

These redshirt transfers led us to two consecutive 20-plus winning seasons and secured two post-season tournament berths—the NIT in the first season and the NCAA tournament the following year. Taking a risk reduction in scholarships paid off in that first year. One of the redshirt transfers was Cedric Jackson, whom I mentioned earlier.

The day after I accepted the position at Cleveland State, I had a conference call with Cedric, his parents, and his high school coach. They had already faxed Cedric's signed release from St. John's University, and they were all but ready to commit to Cleveland State without even seeing any other schools. Cedric was ready to become a Viking.

With only eight players under contract, it was crucial to retain as many returning players as possible. Among them were five seniors, one of whom was a walk-on, and one upperclassman. The rest were sophomores, and there was one signed freshman—all Millennials. We were entering a time when the Millennial Generation was coming to an end.

Even though the end was near, I had come to realize that when you make Millennials part of crafting your program's culture, they'll feel included and valued. And when Millennials feel included and valued, they'll give you their very best. (Chris Tuff, The Millennial Whisperer, paraphrased) J'Nathan Bullock, our team's best player, exemplified this commitment and led us to our first NCAA Tournament appearance in twenty years.

EMERGENCY ROOM SAGA CONTINUES . . .

During the final hours I spent in the emergency room (ER), I had hoped for the same level of commitment and diligence from the doctors. I had spent most of the day waiting for answers, hoping they were giving me their very best. Finally, the last doctor provided an explanation. She revealed that the issue was caused by hemorrhoidal tissue build-up and a burst sack filled with blood, which led to excessive blood flow.

She assured me that the fainting was due to the loss of blood, as mentioned earlier. The doctor expressed confidence that this was the problem and that I would be able to leave the hospital that evening. A specialist had been arranged to see me, and it was expected that the matter would clear up in a short time. The doctor's commitment and diligence in finding the cause of my problem were evident. Thanks to her dedication, I was able to go home a short while later.

Meanwhile, rumblings on campus began to circulate that some players were considering transferring, including our team's best player, J'Nathan Bullock. J'Nathan, a 6'5", 250-pound forward, had been selected to the All-Freshman Team in the Horizon League that season. He had earned two nicknames, J'Nate and Bull, representing both his name and his bullish playing style on the basketball court. In high school, J'Nate had excelled in both football and basketball, garnering All-American status in football and catching the attention of top universities across the country. As news spread about J'Nathan's potential transfer, football schools like

Michigan State, Purdue, and Illinois tried to convince him to switch to their programs.

I had a big task ahead of me: I had to convince J'Nathan to stay at Cleveland State and choose basketball over football. I hoped that the relationships he had developed at the university would help him remain loyal to Cleveland State. Later in my tenure, I faced a similar situation when we tried to recruit another Cleveland-based player, Travis Kelce, who ultimately chose the University of Cincinnati, as his love for football was stronger than his passion for basketball. Travis has since become the best tight end in the NFL, playing for the Kansas City Chiefs and winning three championships.

J'Nathan Bullock

When I had the opportunity to sit down and talk with J'Nathan, I realized that his heart was truly with basketball. My next task was to explain how I could help him develop his skills in the game and support him in reaching the next level. Respect was also crucial to keeping J'Nathan at Cleveland State. Chris Tuff's observations about Millennials craving respect and needing their best interests at heart resonated with me. I understood that providing opportunities for Millennials to succeed on their terms was essential if I wanted to retain their talent. J'Nathan chose to stay at Cleveland State, and he led the team to their first NCAA Tournament appearance in twenty years.

Year one started with great enthusiasm and optimism from the returning players and the newly appointed staff. With only two recruits to bring in, we had more time to focus on campus. However, due to the late recruiting period, finding quality recruits became a challenge. Nonetheless, we were excited about the three players who were redshirting for the following year, which meant our recruiting needs for that year would also be small.

We remained committed to finding the right two Millennials who could contribute in the first year and be assets for years to come. These two players had to be loyal and show allegiance to the cause, as well as be willing to help the program achieve the next level of excellence. Just like

J'Nathan Bullock

building any quality relationship, the Millennial recruitment period is an investment that will pay long-term dividends, as Chris Tuff suggests.

Chapter 11:

CHARACTER UNDERVALUED

"Imagine being undervalued by everybody around you. At one point in time, you stop doing the work or loving people because you know you are taken for granted. On the other hand, if someone appreciates even the tiniest thing you do, you feel like doing more."

—**Bhairavi Sharma**, Author of Mind Cuffed and The Abyssal Secrets

Now, who did we need in that first year that could help Cleveland State be competitive and set the groundwork for the following years? We understood that the Millennial Generation was still at the forefront of all our efforts. But would they have the impact they had when they first emerged?

Our first signee that year was Kevin Francis, originally from Toronto, Canada, via Vincennes University College. Jayson Gee, my top assistant coach, had spotted him early in the recruiting process while he was still on the staff at St. Bonaventure. Jayson recognized Kevin as an outstanding prospect, and we were pleasantly surprised that he hadn't committed to another university. Kevin, one of the older Millennials, had great potential. Standing at 6'8" with solid shooting skills, and being a quality human being as well, he possessed all the attributes that power five conference schools sought. He was a valuable addition, especially since we lacked perimeter shooting.

Next, we signed Joe Davis, a local talent from Cleveland. He had been the city's leading scorer that season, averaging close to 30 points per game. It was astonishing that he was still available. Obviously, the Lord was looking out for us.

Joe had a fearless approach to shooting, reminiscent of Vinny Johnson, the "microwave" of the Detroit Pistons, a two-time NBA Champion during his years, who would heat up and shoot out any team he faced off the bench. He owned the "Six Man" award in the NBA for

Joe Davis

number of years. Joe had that same mindset. He was an instant scoring threat and did not see a shot he would not take!

We also welcomed Breyhon Watson, a transfer from Mott Community College, the number one junior college in Michigan. Breyhon joined us as a preferred walk-on, which meant he received all the benefits of a scholarship player, except for a full-ride scholarship. However, if he met the stipulated requirements, he would earn a full-ride scholarship the following year.

Breyhon exceeded expectations, becoming a starter and earning his scholarship. His character and leadership qualities were evident, and he was also selected to be team captain. Together, these Millennials formed the core of our team, which was now set for the year.

The season began with impressive wins in the non-conference games. We secured an unexpected road victory against Delaware, a team projected to be a frontrunner in their conference. We followed that up with a tournament victory in the America's Youth Classic, defeating Miami of Florida, an ACC contender. The non-conference season concluded with a significant win over Kent State, a program I had previously coached. This was also a program that Cleveland State hadn't beaten in years.

Breyhon Watson

However, we faced a setback during non-conference play when Victor Morris, one of our top scorers and best guards, suffered a foot injury during the Ohio State game. Ohio State eventually reached the Final Four in the NCAA Tournament. Despite this setback, our team maintained their resilience throughout the conference season. Victor later became an assistant coach on my staff a few years after his graduation from Cleveland State.

Our Millennials performed beyond expectations. We focused on their positive attributes, boosting their confidence and eliminating negativity from their past. As Chris Tuff highlighted in *The Millennial Whisperer*, Millennials thrive on inspiration, motivation, and possibility.

This is the primary reason I believe we had this early success. Chris Tuff also says, when "I channeled some of the newfound energy into managing this young team of Millennials, they exceeded my expectations in nearly every conceivable way." Therefore, I cannot leave out the type of character these Millennials also demonstrated throughout the early part of the season; it was outstanding. However, we couldn't take full credit, as most of the players were recruited by the previous staff.

Nevertheless, we understood our primary responsibility was to teach these young players the distinction between right and wrong behavior. As Bruce Tulgan points out in *Not Everyone Gets a Trophy*, Millennials have "giant BS detectors." If you want to teach them about good citizenship, you better not act like a jerk yourself. Our goal was also to instill in them good judgment, which is crucial for character development.

Tulgan emphasizes that "the single most important factor in good judgment is how a person thinks about their life experiences." This was a key aspect of character that I wanted these Millennials to grasp. I encouraged them to ask themselves important questions regarding good judgment, such as, "Do I stop and reflect before making decisions and taking actions?" and "Do I think about cause and effect?" This is how character spreads and takes root among the Millennial Generation.

CHARACTER TRAITS

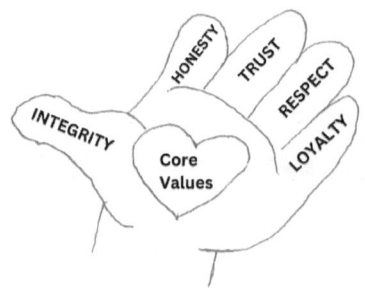

To further emhasize self-evaluation, I encouraged each player to engage in daily self-assessment, reflecting on their behavior. Tulgan highlights that "self-evaluation is not just a key component of learning good judgment. It is the beginning, middle, and end of self-management.

If you teach Millennials one thing, teach them to make a commitment to constant rigorous self-evaluation."

With this in mind, I demanded that every member of the team focus on five Core Values of Character that would help them self-evaluate their behavior and demonstrate good character judgment, according to Siri's definitions:

Integrity: The quality of being honest and having strong moral principles; moral uprightness. Simply put, doing the right thing because it's the right thing to do, regardless of whether anyone is watching. As Simon Sinek highlighted in Leaders Eat Last, integrity goes beyond being honest when we agree with each other; it's about being honest even when we disagree or make mistakes.

Trust: The firm belief in the reliability and truth of someone or something, accepting the truth without evidence or investigation. Trust is earned by being a person others can rely on, following through on our words and actions. As Bruce Schneier explained in Trust and Modern Society, trust is crucial in our interactions with various people, institutions, and systems in modern society.

Honesty: A facet of moral character that connotes positive and virtuous attributes such as integrity, truthfulness, and straightforwardness. It means saying what you mean and being true to your word by telling the truth. As Dr. Brad Blanton highlighted in "Radical Honesty," honesty is essential as lies create stress and ultimately harm us.

Respect: A feeling of deep admiration for someone or something elicited by their abilities, qualities, or achievements. Showing respect means considering others, valuing their words and actions. As Nussein Nishah expressed, respect is about treating people the way you want to be treated and understanding that respect is earned, not given.

Loyalty: A strong feeling of support or allegiance to someone or something. Loyalty means remaining dedicated and committed, giving support regardless of what we receive in return. As Charlie and Tracey Jones stated in *A Message to Millennials*, "Loyalty is something you give regardless of what you get back, and in giving loyalty you're getting more loyalty. And out of loyalty flow other great qualities."

In summarizing these core values, Simon Sinek said, "I have deep loyalty to those who believe integrity is the bedrock of an organization. These beliefs are the making of a very strong culture, one in which the people are committed to one another and to the organization." Therefore, commitment to integrity is essential for any successful program.

As we entered the final six games of the non-conference season, we knew that every core value would be tested. The players' character would face challenges in the classroom, on the basketball court, and in various life situations. I also had to make them understand that they were being held to a higher standard as the flagship program in the athletic department, and their character, judgment, and commitment to evaluating their actions would be on center stage.

With a record of 6-3 in the first nine games, we approached the final stretch with optimism. This was better than anyone expected, even our athletic director.

But just three games in, we lost Victor Morris, one of our top scorers, against Ohio State—a team that ended up in the NCAA Final Four. After that, our season spun out of control and we lost four of the last five non-conference games.

With the conference season about to be at full throttle, we had to pull out all the stops just to compete after being picked to finish last. Then losing leading scorer Kevin Francis due to academic ineligibility was another major setback. Our Millennials wanted to be up to the task at hand, but their capabilities said otherwise.

Still, I felt they competed during each contest and at times showed unbelievable staying power. They never quit, and competed wholeheartedly, no matter what the circumstances were. More than their play, it was their outstanding character that stood out. They displayed good sportsmanship, regardless of whether they won or lost. I was proud to coach these Millennials.

EMERGENCY ROOM SAGA CONTINUES . . .

The emergency room staff who treated me that night showed similar dedication. Despite the chaotic circumstances, they remained committed to providing the best care possible. This encounter will forever be etched in my memory, and that's why I share it in each chapter of this book.

Another aspect that greatly contributed to the rewarding experience of that season was our Success Class, a course I created for our team to take during our personal time. Although not an accredited university course, it played a vital role in boosting the players' confidence and redefining success on their terms. I had them define success as they saw it out of their own eyes, and I would not allow the world to define it for them.

We met once per week for an hour in a relaxed, but focused atmosphere. This class was all about us as a team and no one else. I chose a book each year for us to read and complete; that demonstrated character, leadership, and successful examples. Our objective was to incorporate

John R. Wooden

what we read in the book, into our team philosophy and our daily lives.

The book we used for this particular year was *Pyramid of Success* by John Wooden. Why this book? Because I was trying to create a culture at Cleveland State that defined success in a way which was opposite of the world's definition. Which focused on winning at any cost, while fixated on prestige and accolades, as appose to obtaining success through hard work and honest achievements.

I had each player identify a building block to complete their own personal pyramid. They chose terms like team spirit, loyalty, dedication, commitment, self-control, and character. Once we had our pyramids in place, we set a collective goal for the season: to win the Senior Day game, something Cleveland State hadn't managed in five long years.

Senior Day is a special moment at the end of the season when seniors and their parents or guardians are honored before the game. Parents walk onto the court with their child, the female parent receives flowers, and the whole group gets a round of applause and a photograph. At Cleveland State, we also presented the player with a framed jersey. It's a joyful occasion, a moment of accomplishment, but only if the team wins. For seniors, how they finish their final season often defines their entire college basketball experience. Given our track record, these seniors had little reason to expect a different outcome.

But Success Class changed everything. It gave this team a new mindset and hope for a successful outcome. We went into the Senior Day game determined to make a difference, and we did just that. We defeated the third-ranked team in the conference, and the sense of accomplishment was palpable in the arena. The players were elated, jumping in the air and on the score table as if they had won the conference championship. Success Class had given them something they would carry for the rest of their lives.

Instead of ending the season on a sour note and leaving Cleveland State feeling like failures, these seniors believed they had achieved something meaningful. This belief was so strong that they became the biggest financial supporters of the program and provided unwavering support throughout my tenure at Cleveland State. This is the legacy of Success Class.

Reflecting on the character shown by this group of Millennials during such a challenging season, I realized that character was the true catalyst for our success. That year was a triumph, measured by our own standards, and nothing could take that away from us. Our character never wavered, and it will always be a cornerstone of our program. Cleveland State had arrived, and we were establishing our place in the Horizon League, with character leading the way.

Chapter 12:

TRANSFORMATIONAL LEADERSHIP

"Leadership is about power and the ability to know when and how to use it to influence the people around you to do and become more! Transformational leadership is about using your actions to elevate others and put them on their path to greatness."

—**Terina R. Allen,** President & CEO of Arvis Institute

We knew we were brewing something special in Cleveland. In just our second year, we recruited three freshmen from within the state: Norris Cole from Dayton, D'Aundray Brown from Youngstown, and Eric Schiele from Atwater. It was crucial for us to master recruiting in Ohio, a fertile state for basketball talent.

Eric, a true prodigy from Northeast Ohio, had led the state in scoring during his senior year. Remarkably, he joined Cleveland State as a walk-on, without a scholarship for that year.

Norris Cole

However, it was the two scholarship players, Norris and D'Aundray, who would profoundly impact the trajectory of Cleveland State basketball for the next five years. These two Millennials were the total package: strong leaders, exceptional basketball players, and dedicated students. Just as importantly, they possessed the character values that aligned with our program's culture. Norris and D'Aundray would soon become the faces of Cleveland State Basketball.

D'Aundray Brown

This marked the beginning of our four-year Vision Plan, a carefully crafted blueprint for the program's future. I firmly believed that for any vision to materialize, and have any real meaning, it had to be documented and put into tangible form. I also recognized that a vision is more than just a dream or wish; it requires planning and foresight.

Creating a vision means having the ability to "plan future events with imagination and wisdom." I believed this was a gift granted to me through God's wisdom, enabling me to form a mental image of what the future could be like. Therefore, I documented my envisioned goals for the program over the next four years and shared them with my athletic director, Lee Reed.

While he acknowledged the potential of my plan, he expressed a more modest ambition, stating, "I like what you have created, but this is not necessary. All you need to do is bring this program back to respectability, and I'll be satisfied."

But at the end of two years, an astonishing thing happened. We had achieved an incredible 95% completion rate on the goals I had outlined in the plan. Our vision was rapidly transforming into reality.

The effectiveness of our Vision Plan caught the attention of many coaches in the Midwest, who were amazed by its success and the accuracy of its predictions. While the last two years of the Vision Plan didn't materialize as precisely as we had anticipated, we still managed to achieve 75% of the goals we had set. This meant that over the four-year period, we accomplished at least 85% of the goals outlined in our Vision Plan – an incredible feat.

CLEVELAND STATE BASKETBALL

THE VISION

- Establish Basketball Tradition
- Top 25 Program
- Continue Graduation Success

League Vision

- Top Mid Major League in the Country
- National Tournament Success
- Professional Media Exposure

Program Vision

- New Practice Facilities
- High Major Schedule
- First Class Travel

The foundation for this year's team's success was laid during the summer prior to the school year. Unlike the previous regime, every member of the team was enrolled in summer school for both sessions.

Despite the team's composition primarily consisting of Millennials, our focus remained on identifying the right leaders to unify the group, regardless of generation. We were committed to operating the team with the same ethos as the Marine Corps, embracing the belief that "simply wanting to be a leader and being willing to work is not enough and that "leadership is also a matter of character – not just strength, intelligence or achievement." (*Leaders Eat Last*) This is the code of honor that the Marine Corps upholds.

The coaching staff identified only two players on the team who possessed the necessary qualities and leadership potential to guide the team forward. The first choice was J'Nathan Bullock, who had demonstrated his leadership abilities during the tumultuous first year. He also exhibited impeccable character during difficult moments.

J'Nate, as his teammates affectionately called him, was entering his junior year, and the team would have four additional juniors. These upperclassmen were highly talented and willing to follow the right leader, as long as they could respect him.

J'Nathan Bullock was the ideal choice for team captain due to his ability to influence his teammates both on and off the court. His exemplary character and remarkable transformation in the first year made him well-prepared to assume this leadership responsibility in the second year.

The other team captain, Breyhon Watson, was one of the two seniors on the team and had rightfully earned the opportunity to lead this group of Millennials. He had consistently demonstrated a selfless service mentality, making numerous sacrifices for his teammates. Breyhon's strong character also made him an ideal role model for the team.

He, like J'Nathan, also transformed his leadership skills during that first year. As their coach, I set aside time each week to teach and prepare them on how to be effective leaders. I emphasized the importance of leadership within the overall team dynamic because I didn't want them to underestimate its significance. Simon Sinek echoes this sentiment, stating that "Leadership is a responsibility that hinges almost entirely on character. It's about integrity, honesty, and accountability—all aspects of trust."

He further emphasizes, "In the Marine Corps, trust and integrity are considered matters of life and death." While we at Cleveland State didn't operate under such extreme circumstances, trust remained a cornerstone of our success as a unit.

So, how important was trust to this group of Millennials? These two leaders guided a bunch of hardworking men who trusted each other, like the officers in the Marine Corps, to a higher level of achievement. Cleveland State achieved their first plus 20-win season in the modern age, as well as their first post-season appearance in twenty years under this leadership. They also played for the conference championship and a trip to the NCAA Tournament. I believe the right leadership can successfully transform any organization or unit.

As I mentioned earlier, these Millennials' preparation for success began as early as the summer. I required each player in the program to commit to attending both summer school sessions. This commitment had never been mandated before due to the added financial burden, but our administration was fully invested in this endeavor.

Our goal for the summer, was to have them train hard on the court and in the weight room, move a step closer toward their degrees, and bond together as a unit for the upcoming season. These Millennials embraced this rigorous summer schedule with exceptional dedication.

Their days began with a 6:00 AM weightlifting session, followed by an intensive skill training session after their classes. They ended each day with either open gym or summer league competition. This routine was maintained five days a week for the entire sixteen-week summer period. On those days, there was no room for anything else except homework, eating, and sleeping.

To foster camaraderie, the staff and players ate meals together, both breakfast and dinner. Every aspect of our summer activities was geared towards the success of the upcoming season. The successful outcome of the season served as a testament to the effectiveness of our summer plan and further validated our Vision Plan.

Once all the players returned from their short summer break in the fall, the staff was committed to getting the season off to a strong start. We went on a three-day staff retreat just before the players arrived on campus. During this retreat, held at an isolated location, the staff had the exclusive use of the facility. We stayed overnight to thoroughly assess the year ahead.

I had our academic coordinator, strength coach, and physical trainer meet us at the retreat site on the second day, so we could discuss their philosophies and the programs they would administer throughout the year. As a staff, we engaged in extensive discussions about my vision for the program and the goals we aimed to achieve.

We talked about our academic program, recruiting strategies, strength and conditioning plans, and finally, the basketball-related aspects of the overall program. We conversed about each area in detail with the aid of PowerPoint presentations and notebooks outlining everything we would cover during the season and academic year.

Once we returned from the retreat, our focus shifted to preparing for the arrival of the players. We took great pride in assisting them with the move into their dorms or apartments, taking the opportunity to spend quality time with their parents and anyone accompanying them.

The players arrived on either Friday or Saturday, and the following Sunday, all athletes from each team had mandatory university and athletic orientation meetings. These meetings served as an introduction to campus life and helped them familiarize themselves with their schedules before their first classes began on Monday.

As part of our program commitment, we continued our practice of meeting for breakfast every Monday through Friday as a team. This social gathering served multiple purposes: it provided a nutritious morning meal, fostered team bonding, and allowed players to interact with coaches and teammates before starting their day. This practice laid the foundation for our culture, which was built on teamwork, character, and mutual support.

Once classes were underway, it was time to prepare the players for a successful academic year and a challenging basketball season. Six days after their arrival, we convened a team meeting with the players and the entire staff. The staff included our coaching staff, trainer, academic coordinator, strength and conditioning coaches, basketball operations director, video coordinator, graduate assistants, and student managers.

Each attendee received a comprehensive notebook and materials to organize their responsibilities for the season and year. During this meeting, we also identified the team captains for the season and conducted a formal swearing-in ceremony, upholding a longstanding program tradition. We truly valued the importance of this leadership role within our program.

From the moment we began practicing, I had a strong sense that this team was something special. There was an undeniable sense of camaraderie among the players, and they were all willing to make sacrifices for the well-being of their teammates. The leadership was exactly what I expected, and even more, the two captains took pride in their responsibilities. Equally impressive was the commitment shown by the rest of the players to support the captains and follow their lead, no matter the circumstances.

In their book, *A Message to Millennials*, Charles T. Jones and Tracey C. Jones eloquently articulate the concept of the lead follower: "As a follower, you can serve alongside the leader and, in essence, become the lead follower. The surest path to the leadership chair is through serving at the side of the leader. The lead follower honors the leader and makes him or her look good."

The Joneses further emphasize: "Do this and you will begin the internal transformation to becoming a leader without even realizing it."

Even though we encountered some challenging moments when things didn't go as planned, the steadfast leadership displayed by our captains kept us on track towards our goals and made our Vision Plan seem even more attainable.

We kicked off the season's non-conference portion with great enthusiasm and confidence. I knew we would catch many teams off guard because Cleveland State hadn't been on anyone's radar for quite some time. We had some significant wins in the non-conference schedule, including victories over South Florida of the Big East Conference and Florida State of the ACC. However, we also experienced some narrow defeats against George Mason and Georgia Southern. As the non-conference play came to an end, we faced two tough losses against Ohio

State of the Big Ten and Kent State representing the Mid-American Conference.

It's worth noting that both Ohio State and Kent State went on to win their respective conferences and participate in the NCAA Tournament. Overall, I considered our non-conference season a success, and it provided us with the momentum we needed to compete in the Horizon League.

Like the non-conference teams, the Horizon League teams had no idea of the challenge they were about to face when going up against our team. We started conference play with an impressive six-game winning streak before experiencing our first setback on the road. One of those six victories included Butler, who was the preseason favorite to win the conference. Our initial encounter with Butler took place at the Henry J. Goodman Arena, also known as the Wolstein Center, home of the Cleveland State Vikings.

CSU Championship

This was the first time Cleveland State had defeated Butler since their entry into the league, and we did so convincingly. The atmosphere was electrifying, as we had close to 10,000 fans in attendance. Our trainer who had been at Cleveland State for a number of years said, "This arena has not looked and felt like this in years."

Our performance that evening sparked a renewed sense of excitement among Cleveland's basketball fans. As one long-time fan put it after the game, "We finally have a team worth supporting, a team worth following all the way to the finish line." I witnessed a group of Millennials poised to accomplish something extraordinary, something that hadn't been done in a long time.

Heading into the second half of league play, we traveled to Butler with the opportunity to take the conference lead with only four games remaining. However, it was not to be. They edged us out in a close, down-to-the-wire game. Nevertheless, we finished the season with an impressive twelve league wins, the most Cleveland State had ever achieved in the Horizon League.

The leadership was outstanding throughout the year, and it was truly shown down the stretch when these youthful Millennials needed it the most. We carried this momentum into the Horizon League Tournament and won our semi-final contest against Valparaiso for the first time. This victory set us up for a third-time encounter with Butler, with a trip to the NCAA Tournament on the line.

In a hard-fought battle at Hinkle Fieldhouse, their home court and the filming location of the iconic movie "Hoosiers," Butler prevailed, capturing the conference championship. While disappointment was inevitable, this ending wasn't too shabby for a group of Millennials in their first year together. I knew in that moment that this was just the beginning, and these millennials would make their mark again in the future. Their legacy was just beginning.

Hinkle Fieldhouse

EMERGENCY ROOM SAGA CONTINUES . . .

Drawing parallels between this basketball season and my experience in the Tampa General Hospital Emergency Room, I can appreciate that neither situation was as bad as I initially thought. Being thrust into such a challenging situation, facing unforeseen circumstances, and being under the care of so many Millennials, I gained a deeper understanding of the pressures this generation faces daily.

Yet, the leadership I encountered from the doctors was truly transformative. They helped me get through some difficult moments and I left the hospital feeling confident that I had received the best possible care.

Similarly, this team played to the best of their abilities throughout the season. But there was more in store for us. With our overall record, we qualified for a post-season tournament: the National Invitation Tournament (NIT). The NIT still held prestige, and teams reveled in the privilege of being selected to play in New York at Madison Square Garden, the iconic arena I mentioned earlier in the chapters. We jumped at the opportunity for that experience.

In the early rounds of the NIT, games were played at the higher-seeded team's home site, giving them a distinct advantage. We were selected to play against Dayton, the 5th seeded team from the Atlantic Ten Conference (A10). Dayton finished 4th in the strong A10 Conference that season. The matchup against another Ohio school was unique, as it allowed our fans to easily support the team.

We played well in the first half, but Dayton outlasted us in the second half, advancing to the next round of the tournament. However, the experience gained from playing in the NIT was invaluable, and I knew it would benefit us in the following year. And indeed, one year later, we won the conference championship and received an NCAA Tournament bid for the first time in twenty years at Cleveland State.

Nonetheless, the Vikings ended this season with 21 wins, placing us in a league of our own. We were one of only 16 teams in NCAA College Division 1 Basketball history to go from losing 20 or more games in their first season to winning 20 or more games in the next season. This achievement put us in rare company. However, I must truly credit the leadership provided by the captains throughout the year as the primary reason for the success and turnaround of this group of character-driven Millennials.

Our team included five seniors who would become our first graduating class at Cleveland State, though Chris Moore, one of the seniors, is not shown in the photo. Maintaining a tradition I held dear throughout my tenure at Cleveland State University, all our seniors successfully graduated during my time.

Graduate Seniors

These five seniors set the stage of excellence for the future Millennials to follow in their footsteps. As Molly Friedenfield, author of *The Book of Simple Truths* once said, "When your footsteps and thoughts carry you down the same path your heart and soul are directing, you will know without a doubt that you are headed in the right direction." These Millennials knew without a doubt they were headed in the right direction.

In that second year, we transformed the entire program, and I firmly believe our leadership was the catalyst. Our basketball game evolved into a well-oiled machine, which was evident with the turnaround at the season's end.

Finally, our character played a major role in the transformation of this team. We represented our moral and ethical values, and that became an integral part of our identity. In essence, we became a character-driven unit, focusing not just on our accomplishments, although we did achieve a great deal in that second year. These Millennials never lost sight of the importance of character and leadership as the crux of our identity.

Chapter 13:

MILLENNIAL EXPANSION

"Ever since I was a child I have had this instinctive urge for expansion and growth. To me, the function and duty of a quality human being is the sincere and honest development of one's potential."

—**Bruce Lee,** American Martial Artist & Actor

Where does Cleveland State go from here? In my mind, and the minds of many around the city of Cleveland, we were headed to the next level of college basketball, a level that only a few schools have a chance to experience. The last time Cleveland State experienced such progress was back in 1986, when they beat the Naval Academy in the NCAA Regional Finals, featuring the great David

CSU Team Photo

Robinson, on their way to an NCAA Sweet Sixteen appearance.

The program was expanding in all phases of its existence, with the Millennials leading the charge. We were entering our third year, and expectations were soaring, leaving no room for deceleration. As the old saying goes, "When you're at the bottom, there's nowhere to go but up." In our case, there was only one direction – to the very top!

Like the previous year, we knew this summer would be as important to our success as any time of the season. Once again, we were committed to being on campus the entire summer, but for a different reason. We were scheduled to go on a foreign tour of Spain to compete against professional competition at the end of the summer.

This trip would be sponsored by Fifth Third Bank, a financial booster for the program. In return, all they asked of us was to observe the banking system in Spain and report back to them on their operational procedures. We identified two players on the team who were business majors and willing to take on the responsibility of completing this task.

To be eligible for the foreign trip, players had to meet specific requirements under NCAA regulations. College teams embarking on foreign tours were allowed up to 10 separate days of full operational practices before the trip, in addition to the designated weekly hours for skill training.

Additionally, players had to complete at least 6 successful hours of coursework during the summer to be eligible. These requirements were not only important for the foreign trip but also for their overall academic, physical, and basketball development for the upcoming season.

We trained and practiced rigorously throughout the sixteen weeks of summer, preparing ourselves for the professional competition we would face on the foreign trip. However, the trip meant more than just an athletic competition to us. As a staff and as players, we saw it as an opportunity to grow and mature as a unit, strengthening our bond as a family and team.

The tour proved to be an exceptional experience for everyone involved. My wife, the coaching staff, other staff members, the players, and the family members who accompanied us to support the team thoroughly enjoyed the journey. We traveled to and played in three different cities in Spain: Madrid, Valencia, and Barcelona.

Madrid, the capital, was the first city we visited, which had a great deal of historical scenery surrounding it, as well as preserved ancient sites. The most fascinating attraction was an actual bullfighting arena. The players and family members were noticeably shocked and surprised by the brutality of the bullfight. The matador overpowered the bull and once the bull surrendered, the matador delivered the final strike, stabbing the bull between the eyes with a saber right in front of us. This moment was undeniably intense and traumatic, leaving a lasting impression on many of us.

Charlie Jones, in his book *A Message to Millennials*, aptly observes: "Every time you expose yourself to a new situation, it'll give you another key of experience for your key ring." He continues, "Soon the key ring begins to fill with experiences, and we learn to pick the right key to unlock any situation." After witnessing this spectacle, most of these Millennials decided it was a situation they never wanted to experience again; a door they preferred to keep locked.

Our next stop, Valencia, offered a delightful change of pace with its coastal charm. The city is renowned for its stunning beaches with pristine white sand and turquoise waters. It was a picturesque scene that will forever be etched in my memory. We were there for two days and when we weren't playing basketball, we were at the beach enjoying the water. Our second game took place on the outskirts of town, yet the crowd attendance remained remarkable. People flocked to the arena as if we were the sole attraction in all of Spain. The atmosphere was electric, and we relished the spirited competition.

Valencia also offered a charming small-town atmosphere; quaint places were scattered throughout the town for us to explore and appreciate. It was such an enchanting sight that my wife and I promised each other that we would return in the near future.

The final leg of our 10-day trip brought us to Barcelona, the largest city in Spain. This was the same city that hosted the 1992 Olympic Games, where the legendary United States Dream Team, the greatest basketball roster ever assembled, made their mark. Throughout our time in Barcelona, we visited numerous sites that were constructed for the Olympic Games. We even had the privilege of playing our two games on the very same court where the Dream Team showcased their talent.

When we weren't playing games, we were immersing ourselves in the vibrant culture of Barcelona, one of Europe's most historically significant cities. One sight that left an indelible mark on my wife and me was the Basilica de la Sagrada Familia, one of Europe's most captivating churches.

Basilica de la Sagrada Familia

The intricately carved details both inside and outside the massive structure were truly inspiring.

The architects and builders have been working on this masterpiece since 1882, and its completion is scheduled for 2026. The renowned architect Antoni Gaudi was the initial visionary behind the Sagrada Familia, and his impact on European history is widely recognized.

Our foreign tour proved to be an exceptional experience, strengthening our bond as a team and a family. We won all five games we played against the professional teams, which was the primary reason I wanted us to go on this foreign tour. My research indicated that teams that participate in foreign tours prior to their season experience an 80% or higher success rate.

This trip also provided us with invaluable insights into Spanish culture, giving our millennial players a firsthand experience of how another country operates and lives within its political structure. We also dedicated significant time during the trip to strengthen our bond as a unit.

One unforgettable moment occurred on a hotel rooftop in Madrid, where we shared a special night together as a team, away from the rest of the traveling group. Underneath a fluorescent blue sky adorned with twinkling stars, a sight that figuratively took our breath away, we truly connected as a team.

This special moment turned out to be even more significant than we could have imagined, as it played a crucial role in uniting this group of millennials and fueling their remarkable success throughout the year. The foreign trip exposed us to the expanding potential of our program and demonstrated the extensive growth within our millennial players.

Shortly after our return to the states, the fall semester began, and we had to transition back to the academic grind. We carried the momentum and growth we had established in Spain into our pre-season conditioning and early practices. It was evident to me that this group had advanced and developed significantly due to the experiences they gained on the foreign tour.

The pre-season media day, held in Chicago, Illinois, during the first week of October, brought exciting news. Cleveland State was selected as the pre-season favorite to win the Horizon League championship and secure an automatic berth in the NCAA Tournament.

Two players from our team, J'Nathan Bullock and Cedric Jackson, were chosen to attend Media Day alongside me. J'Nathan was the frontrunner for pre-season player of the year, while Cedric joined him on the pre-season all-conference team. We left Chicago that evening with a heightened sense of pride, feeling like we belonged among the conference's elite. This was a feeling that Cleveland State had not experienced in years.

Despite the pre-season accolades, we couldn't allow pride to cloud our judgment, because we hadn't played a single game of the season. But on that night, we were considered to be the best team in the Horizon League. This signified a remarkable turnaround for these Millennials, who had elevated their presence not only within the Horizon League but also on the national stage. Just two years prior, Cleveland State had been picked last in the Horizon League. Now, we were poised atop the tenth-best conference in Division I men's basketball.

Back in Cleveland, the season was underway, and every step forward brought us closer to our ultimate goal of winning the Horizon League championship and securing a berth in the NCAA post-season tournament. Achieving this feat would align perfectly with the objectives of our Vision Plan.

I immediately met with my staff to make sure everyone understood the magnitude of the challenge we were about to face. We had to accept that every team on our schedule would be bringing their "A-game" every time we stepped onto the court. This meant that we had to perform at our absolute best every game, leaving no room for error.

The non-conference schedule was filled with highly competitive teams, many of whom were also favored to win their respective conference championships. We embraced the challenge and started the non-conference portion of the season strongly, winning eleven out of the fourteen games played.

The three losses came against Power 5 schools, such as the University of Washington and Kansas State, both of whom participated in the NCAA Tournament that season. We also faced the University of West Virginia, a nationally ranked team. The game against West Virginia, played at their arena, was a closely contested battle that came down to the final seconds, with us having a chance to steal a victory.

Despite these losses, we secured a significant non-conference win over Syracuse University, who was ranked No. 5 in the country at the time. This victory made national headlines as Cedric Jackson hit a buzzer-beating 60-footer to secure the win. Our overall performance in the non-conference season demonstrated that we were on a trajectory that would be difficult for our league opponents to stop.

Syracuse Arena

We had a strong start to the conference season, no doubt, but reality hit us hard in the second game when we lost a nail-biter to Butler on our home court. At the time, Butler was coached by Brad Stevens, who later became the head coach of the Boston Celtics. I will never forget the shot that sealed our fate. With Cleveland State up by one point and two seconds remaining on the clock, Butler's best long-range shooter launched a 40-footer from beyond the center circle. The buzzer-beating shot sent shockwaves through the capacity crowd, leaving everyone in disbelief. At that moment, I couldn't help but think back to the Syracuse game and thought to myself, "What karma!"

Throughout the conference season, we fluctuated between first and third place, with a chance to compete for the regular season conference championship. The biggest obstacle in our path was the final game of the regular season, scheduled to be played at Butler's Fieldhouse. Despite knowing this from the beginning, we found ourselves in a hard-fought contest, ultimately losing by two points in the hostile environment of Hinkle Fieldhouse. Little did we know at the time that this would be a similar situation we would face again, but with a different outcome.

I vividly recall a soul-searching moment on the bus ride back to Cleveland after that last regular-season game. All the coaches were sitting in the front, as we usually did, along with Lee Reed. This was the first time that season Lee had traveled on the bus with us. Lee engaged in an emotional conversation with two of my assistant coaches, expressing his feelings about the season and how we had let a great opportunity slip away. He knew that if we had won that last game, even though it would have resulted in a tie for the regular season title, we would have won the tiebreaker, securing home court advantage and a bye in the first round of the Horizon League Tournament. I could sense the disappointment in his words.

After Lee's assessment, I delivered a statement that stunned him into momentary silence. I looked at him and said, "I know we will win the conference championship and go to the NCAA Tournament." My statement was direct, devoid of emotion, and delivered with unwavering conviction. I followed it up by saying, "I now know how we will beat them. We had to go through this, in order to accomplish what we are about to accomplish."

Indeed, I realized that to give Butler a different look and throw them off, we needed to make some changes and adjustments. I kept that information in mind and put it on the shelf, waiting for the championship game against Butler.

Lee, still struggling with the past defeat, didn't know what to say. He understood that winning at Hinkle Fieldhouse, where Butler had not lost a single league game all season, would be a daunting task. However, I remained confident that we could overcome the odds and achieve the unthinkable. Bruce Tulgan's words from his book, *Not Everyone Gets a Trophy*, echoed in my mind: "If you teach Millennials to apply the lessons-learned process to every 'mission' they undertake or to every move they make, the outcome can often be considerably different."

We entered the Horizon League Tournament tied for second place with Wisconsin Green Bay, but our two losses to Butler cost us the tiebreaker. Consequently, we were forced to navigate the longer route to the championship without the automatic bye granted to the first and second-place teams in the first round. This meant we had to win three games in seven days before facing Butler in the championship match. However, if we wanted to make this match-up a reality, we also had to defeat Green Bay in the semifinals.

We handled our first-round game with relative ease, defeating Detroit-Mercy by thirteen points on our home court. The remaining rounds of the tournament would be played at Hinkle Fieldhouse, the Butler Bulldogs' home court, as Butler's reward for winning the regular-season

Championship Game

championship. Our second-round game against Illinois-Chicago was another game that came down to the wire, but we secured the win.

This victory led us to the semifinal matchup against Wisconsin Green Bay, a team we had split games with during the regular season, with each team winning a close contest on their home court. Once again, the game went down to the wire, but Cleveland State surged in the final three minutes to overtake the talented Green Bay Phoenix.

The stage was set for one of the most memorable championship games in Horizon League history. In front of Butler's capacity crowd and on national television, the Cleveland State Vikings defeated the Butler Bulldogs, securing their first Horizon League Championship in Viking history. It was the perfect venue for Cleveland State to gain national recognition and expand the horizons of the millennial generation. This victory will be remembered throughout the annals of Horizon League play.

With the victory celebrations behind us, we turned our attention to the NCAA Tournament selection show, which was scheduled for the final Sunday before the tournament's commencement. The Cleveland State administration went all out for the occasion, organizing a spectacular selection show extravaganza. I had been involved in numerous selection show productions, but none of them matched the scale of this one. Boosters, faculty, staff, administrators, and various media outlets were invited to join the Cleveland State Vikings in celebrating this momentous occasion.

Nearly 200 enthusiastic supporters took advantage of this opportunity, filling all three floors of the Wolstein Center, the Vikings' home court facility. Media outlets set up their stations on the second floor to interview the president, athletic director, players, and basketball coaches. The event was broadcast on four television networks and aired on multiple radio stations.

The third floor, which also housed the entertainment loge overlooking the basketball arena, provided refreshments and catered food that covered the entire area. Additionally, numerous TV monitors were positioned throughout the third floor for viewing the selection show. The basketball staff, team members, and coaches watched the show on a large TV screen in the player's lounge on the bottom floor, while the other guests observed the show on the second and third floors.

A select number of preferred guests, including parents, coaches' family members, and close friends, were also invited to share this moment with the team. The event went off perfectly, and we were thrilled to learn that we would be playing against the Wake Forest Demon Deacons in the first round. Wake Forest was one of the higher-ranked teams in the country, and this presented us with an opportunity to shock the basketball world. Our victory over the Demon Deacons that night is still considered one of the biggest upsets in NCAA Tournament history. We not only defeated them, but we also handed them one of their worst losses of the season.

Unfortunately, our journey came to an end in the Regional Finals with a hard-fought loss to the University of Arizona, another highly ranked team. We were so close to reaching the Sweet 16 of the NCAA

Tournament. The only other Cleveland State team to achieve this feat was the 1986 team, which I mentioned at the beginning of this chapter.

EMERGENCY ROOM SAGA CONCLUSION . . .

Now, how does this season equate with the emergency room experience I encountered at Tampa General Hospital over a decade later? The pressures were immense throughout the season, as we faced challenges at every turn and were uncertain of the outcome. Similarly, the pressures in the hospital came with many challenges, and the Millennials I encountered in the ER did not make matters any easier.

Despite the uncertainties, both experiences yielded remarkable results. The effort I put in during my short stay in the hospital was equivalent to the effort exhibited by this group of Millennials in the NCAA Tournament. Both experiences were unpredictable but ultimately ended in resounding success.

Having completed this chapter, I am left with a fundamental question: did these Millennials expand their presence and undergo significant growth during their first three years at Cleveland State? Without a doubt, the answer is yes. And I believe that this expansion was merely the beginning.

As for how far these Millennials will go and where they will end up, I cannot say for certain. However, if this year is any indication of the potential of the Millennial Generation, then their future is boundless.

Malcolm Harris says in his book, *Kids These Days: Human Capital and the Making of Millennials*, "If Millennials are going to alter the path that we're on, it's realistically going to happen in the next ten to twenty years." Reflecting on my early days at Cleveland State and the Vision Plan I had for this group of Millennials, I am amazed to see that it came to fruition within that timeframe.

Cleveland State's entire program underwent significant expansion, encompassing recruiting, scheduling, training table, tournament appearances, foreign trips, budget increases, charter flights, and numerous other improvements over that ten-year period. We became a program that the city of Cleveland was proud of, and the expansion and advancement of our program were evident to everyone involved.

A MISUNDERSTOOD GENERATION

"Misunderstood, you feel like you don't belong. You observe this society and you question its direction. You look around and see pain, confusion and hate. You simply can't understand why this generation is hell bent on avoiding love, communication, and genuine connection."

—**Sylvester McNutt,** American Author

During a basketball clinic, I once overheard someone make a thought-provoking comment. "Being misunderstood doesn't mean you're the issue. Sometimes it's the people who misunderstand you with all the issues."

I spent five years at Rutgers and eleven years at Cleveland State trying to understand the impact this Millennial Generation was having on the basketball profession, as well as the entire world.

It's important to note that this book primarily focuses on my coaching experiences at Rutgers and only covers a small portion of my time at Cleveland State, specifically between 2000 and 2009. However, the influence of the Millennial Generation extends far beyond that timeframe, and they continue to make a significant impact today, just as they did in those earlier years.

In *Leaders Eat Last* says, Simon Sinek identifies three key factors that have shaped and continue to shape Millennials: over-parenting, ubiquitous technology, and increased opportunities for instant gratification. The effects of these factors are exacerbated by and sometimes conflict with the environments Millennials now navigate, be it in college settings or their professional lives.

Now, the Millennial Generation has shifted and transformed into something different and even more advanced. They are now recognized as Generation Z or the Post-Millennials. Generation Z is commonly defined as individuals born between 1996 and the early to mid-2000s, although the end date can vary depending on the source. Generation Z, with around 90 million individuals, and Millennials, with about 80 million, constitute the two most populous generations ever recorded. This distinction emphasizes their significant influence and impact on society.

What sets Generation Z apart from their predecessors? According to an article by Michael Dimock, "Defining Generations: Where Millennials End and Gen Z Begins," there are three factors. One, they are the first generation to have been entirely immersed in the digital world, and some of them have already entered the workforce. This digital upbringing has shaped their worldview and communication styles.

Two, Generation Z represents the second wave of Millennials, and unlike previous generations, they can have parents from different generations. This means that their parents have passed on their own core values to them, potentially leading to a different ideology and perspective.

And three, Generation Z boasts the highest racial and ethnic diversity of any generation and is projected to be the most educated to date.

Additionally, they are digital natives, with little or no recollection of a pre-smartphone era. While Millennials and Gen Z may appear similar in age, their approaches to life and interactions are remarkably distinct, according to Kim Parker and Ruth Igielnik, in their article, "On the Cusp of Adulthood and Facing an Uncertain Future: What We know about Gen Z So Far." Millennials and Gen Z may look and seem similar in age, but they are considerably different in how they interact and view life.

Senior Class - Players

Fresh off one of the most successful seasons in Cleveland State history, we were about to begin our fourth year. However, we had lost six key players to graduation, including J'Nathan Bullock, Cedric Jackson, George Tandy, Chris Moore, and Renard Fields—five of whom had amassed the most playing time on the court the previous year. This group of Millennials were ready to take the world by storm and establish themselves as leaders in their chosen profession, but we now faced the challenge of replacing them.

To ensure immediate impact, we sought experienced Millennials from the junior college (JC) ranks. We dedicated countless hours scouring the JC circuit for players with the necessary skills and experience to maintain our winning trajectory. However, venturing into the JC arena was not our preferred approach, as past experiences had shown it to be a less fruitful recruiting ground. Our philosophy revolved around building from the ground up, emphasizing teaching, development, and growth. Recruiting talented players directly from high school remained our preferred strategy.

Despite our preference for recruiting directly from high school, because of the loss of so many talented players to graduation it was crucial for us to bring in new players who could step in and contribute immediately. We needed individuals who could hit the ground running and make an immediate impact on our team. Considering this, the junior college route seemed like the best option. However, past experiences have taught me that recruiting junior college players can come with its own set of challenges, especially considering the unique circumstances and characteristics of the Millennial Generation.

We decided to sign three highly sought-after junior college players who had attracted interest from colleges across the country. Additionally,

Aaron Pogue

in the previous year, we had taken a chance on two other transfer players from junior colleges. These players were Aaron Pogue from Dayton, Ohio, and Nigel Ajere from Aradia, California. Both of them had to redshirt that year, and they also had some personal baggage. However, because we had built our program around a strong culture that emphasized character, trust, and hard work, we believed we could help them mature and grow under our guidance.

Interestingly, both Pogue and Ajere had been high school teammates with some of our current players, which we believed could be a significant advantage in helping them adapt to our environment. Nevertheless, dealing with misunderstood Millennials is never without its challenges, as their tendency to deviate from the status quo can sometimes lead to unpredictable situations.

Nigel had a strong bond with Trey Harmon, one of our key players and a starting guard. Trey played a significant role in encouraging Nigel to join our team and assisted us in the recruitment process. Similarly, Aaron, who had been a McDonald's All-American in high school, had a familiar teammate in Norris Cole, the leader of our team. Having these existing players on the team who were familiar with Nigel and Aaron's backgrounds gave us some assurance that they would be looked after and mentored in our culture.

The three other junior college signees came with strong basketball reputations, but questionable character backgrounds as well. Although they had not been involved in any major incidents, there were underlying issues that warranted attention. Junior college players often enjoy a lot of freedom in unsupervised settings, which can lead to hidden problems that even their JC coaches may not know about. We believed that our culture and our existing players could deal with most of these behind-the-scenes issues. However, we also realized that we were taking a gamble by bringing in so many JC players at once, each with their own challenges.

So, did we have a clear understanding of the challenges and experiences of this? Not completely, but we were about to experience it firsthand and throughout the year.

Our top junior college recruit was Lance James, a JC All-American from Aiken Tech in South Carolina. He was followed by Jared Cunningham, a 6'9" shooting forward from Arkansas Fort Smith. The final junior college recruit was Kevin Anderson, a 6'10" post player from the Technical Career Institute (TCI) in New York City.

Lance James

With these three incoming junior college transfers, combined with the two from the previous year, our team now had a total of five junior college players, making up a third of our roster. Having so many junior college players at once raised a major concern for me. I worried that it could create an imbalance within the team, potentially disrupting the harmony we had worked hard to establish. I knew we'd need to do our best to properly manage this team to avoid our culture falling out of balance.

Simon Sinek's concept of 'destructive abundance' resonated with me. He explained that when selfish pursuits outweigh selfless ones, it can lead

Jared Cunningham &
Jeremy Montgomery

to negative consequences. This is exactly what happened with our team of Millennials. They became overly focused on personal goals, forgetting the core values of teamwork and sportsmanship.

It was hard to understand at the time, but "whenever you try to create a 'quick fix' without putting character at the forefront, negative outcomes can occur, even when the motives are sincere." (Waters Words of Wisdom) So, what do the experts mean when they say that this generation is misunderstood? I summarize it in one word: "myths." These myths are like misrepresentations of the truth that are difficult for Millennials to shake off. For example, Chris Tuff (*The Millennials Whisperer*), says some people think of Millennials as "entitled, avocado-toast-eating, Ping-Pong playing, craft-beer-drinking, Game-of-Thrones-watching, unprepared, pessimistic slackers, who are overly reliant on their parents."

Further, in Bruce Tulgan's book, *Not Everyone Gets a Trophy: How to Manage the Millennials*, I came across five prominent myths regarding this generation.

Myth One: "Millennials are disloyal and unwilling to make real commitments."

Reality: Millennials can be extremely loyal, but their loyalty is based on trust and respect, not blind obedience. They appreciate leaders who genuinely care for them and demonstrate sincere intentions. When they feel valued and respected, Millennials become fiercely loyal supporters.

Myth Two: "Millennials don't know as much as they think they do and have short attention spans."

Reality: While Millennials may not possess the same depth of shared knowledge and experience as previous generations, they are incredibly well-informed and have access to an unprecedented amount of information at their fingertips. They are accustomed to thinking, learning, and communicating in sync with today's fast-paced information environment. Their shorter attention spans stem from their exposure to rapid-fire information consumption, leading to occasional impatience.

Myth Three: "Millennials need work to be fun."

Reality: Millennials are not seeking constant entertainment; they crave meaningful work that engages them intellectually and challenges them to grow. They want to understand how their individual contributions align with the broader goals of the organization. When they are genuinely interested in their work, their focus and dedication are unparalleled. As Marc Anthony famously said, "When you do what you love, you'll never work a day in your life."

Myth Four: "Millennials want their coaches/leaders to do their work for them."

Reality: Millennials desire coaches and leaders who invest time in teaching them how to perform their tasks efficiently and effectively. They value guidance and mentorship and when they are engaged and motivated, their work ethic is unparalleled.

Myth Five: "Millennials don't respect their elders."

Reality: On the contrary, they do respect their elders. In fact, they often have closer relationships with their parents and grandparents compared to previous generations. However, they also desire respect in return. Growing up, their parents, teachers, and counselors treated them with respect, and they expect the same from their coaches and leaders. However, they have been taught to avoid direct confrontation with authority figures, and often deferred to their parents to address conflicts.

These Millennial myths might have a sliver of truth, but when you actually work with Millennials, you realize how distorted and misleading they are. Looking back on that season with those junior college

Millennials, it hit me – we didn't prioritize character when we recruited them. We were blinded by their talent, desperate to stay on top, neglecting that crucial ingredient.

Fortunately, we had Norris Cole and D'Aundray Brown leading the way, and we had a solid group of underclassmen and outstanding freshmen who exemplified our character culture. In fact, this collective of Millennials would later become part of the team that achieved the highest number of victories in the program's history. Still, we thought these JC transfers could be the difference-makers – if they developed into the quality individuals we expected them to be.

The non-conference schedule was a beast with the likes of Kentucky, Wichita State, West Virginia, Ohio State, Kansas State and St. Bonaventure, a gauntlet of Power 5 schools. We were David facing multiple Goliaths, and we struggled. Adding to the difficulty was the fact that the majority of these non-conference power games were played on the opponents' home courts or at neutral sites in pre-season tournaments. We only had one opportunity to face one of these teams on our home court. Know that old saying, "Sometimes you bite off more than you can chew"? That was us. The non-conference schedule we created was too demanding, especially for the incoming junior college transfers who had to learn everything from scratch.

It took a whole season to get them up to speed. These weren't skill-less rookies, mind you. These guys had talent. They competed and contributed and helped when they could. We were pushing them, pushing ourselves, to adapt, to overcome. It wasn't pretty. The learning curve was a cliff, and their past histories cast long shadows. But we had made our bed, and we were committed to lying in it, even if it meant some sleepless nights.

So, what kept us going? What kept me from ripping out my hair during practice meltdowns and late-night phone calls?

Their connection. Not just to our team, but to something bigger, a web woven across the country. Tim Elmore called it the "Generation iY" phenomenon – a shared spirit, a community forged in challenges and technology. They understood each other in a way I couldn't, their laughter echoing across continents, their shared attitudes and ideas uniting them through screens.

It was a wild ride, for sure. But that connection became our lifeline. These Millennials, the new and old, the transfers and the homegrown talent, found a way to connect and in doing so, created a bond built on perseverance and trust.

It is a year stamped in my memory, a season of sweat, tears, and triumphs, evidence of the collective power of the human spirit's ability to rise above myths and expectations. And while the non-conference schedule was a brutal teacher, I believed it would prepare us for the conference season and beyond, and I was right. We finished strong, a testament to the lessons learned, the connections forged.

The following year, with the core of that team intact, we soared. We amassed ten wins in the league, one of the highest total wins in school history and a significant accomplishment for that time. It was the culmination of a journey that began with facing our mistakes, embracing the complexities of a generation, and ultimately, believing in their unbreakable bond.

So, yes, the myths about Millennials may hold some truth. But beneath the surface, there's a fire, a loyalty, a connection that defies definition. And as coaches, as leaders, the greatest privilege is not just to witness it, but to nurture it, to watch it light the way to a future that gleams brighter than any championship medal or trophy. We also learned another lesson that year: sometimes, the toughest challenges lead to the sweetest victories.

So, did these Millennial transfers ever find their footing to fit with the program we'd designed? Well, if you just looked at the win-loss record, you might think they did. But when the dust settled, the coaches and four transfers decided it was time to part ways. Turns out, even when you've had some success, finding your true path means knowing when to walk away from the one you're on, even if the path you're on is paved with past achievement. We all agreed they needed a program that better understood their rhythm, a place where they could truly flourish.

We agreed that it would be better for them to transfer into another program, a program that would be more suited to their needs. When you feel misunderstood, sometimes you may have to go your own separate ways, regardless of the success you have obtained. Having a clear understanding of where you have to go, and what it will take to get there is the most important decision, a decision that we mutually agreed upon.

Aaron Pogue

The one JC transfer who stayed? Aaron Pogue. And man, did his career blossom. Those two years became the best of his career. He graduated on time, a scholar athlete, proving to everyone who'd written him off that a misunderstood Millennial with a checkered past could still win.

See, Aaron was the underdog from day one. No one believed in him, but he had this fire in his belly. Hard work, discipline, and a coach who saw his potential—that's what it took for Aaron to rewrite his story. Sure, he needed a lot of support, but he embraced the challenge, grew as a man, and emerged a champion.

It has been said that Millennials had to navigate more cultural shifts than any generation before them. In *The Millennial Whisperer*, Chris Tuff says, "The Younger Millennials didn't experience change in the same way as their older counterparts. They grew up with cell phones and iPods. By the time they were hitting adolescence, smart phones were a staple."

That cultural and technological gap made it hard for older generations to understand what these kids were going through. And older folks, well, they haven't exactly adapted as fast. One thing's for sure, though: the older generation must come to understand this. Millennials crave meaning, purpose, variety, things that keep their fire burning, so that they stay engaged with their work, just as much, if not more than their generational predecessors. They're not robots programmed to fit in pre-made molds. They're individuals, each with their own story to write. And if those of us in older cohorts don't get this, we'll only widen the gap.

So, I still had a few burning questions about these Millennials. Coaching them on the court was one thing because sure, I knew the X's and O's, but understanding them? That was a different ball game. So, I dug in, researched, and here's what I learned:

1. Connection is their currency. Forget fancy facilities, what drives Millennials is the desire for meaningful relationships. They thrive when they feel like they are part of a team, not just a name on a roster.

2. The parental conundrum: Parents can be either the wind beneath their wings or the helicopter hovering overhead. Navigating these dynamics can be a challenge, as Millennials' personal aspirations can clash with parental expectations.

3. They are tech natives. Born in a digital era, Millennials are tech-savvy through and through. They speak the language of the internet fluently. Google, TikTok, Instagram, they're not just platforms, they're wired into how they express, how they connect, and how they navigate the world.

4. They are validation seekers: In a world craving recognition, Millennials are no exception. They yearn for that pat on the back, the nod to a job well done after every drill, every effort exerted. For them, it's not about feeding their egos; it's about feeling seen, appreciated, and valued. The notion of participation trophies resonates with them because they believe that showing up and giving their all deserves recognition.

5. They are prone to self-doubt: Millennials often harbor a built-in fear mechanism that can at times lead them to self-destructive behaviors. This fear, whether it stems from societal pressures or internal insecurities, can impact their decision-making, and hinder their progress.

All the knowledge and awareness I gained through my research on Millennials has deepened my understanding of how this generation functions and operates within our society and the world today. However, even with this newfound understanding, I still find myself grappling with the nuances of this generation. It is intriguing to witness how many

Millennials have ventured into the basketball profession as coaches and have embraced leadership roles in our society. This leads me to pose a question to these Millennial coaches: Do you possess the character and fortitude required to guide the new generation, the Gen Z's, as we navigate our way into an ever-evolving world?

Chris Tuff further says, "Everyone is now talking about the Generation Z that is following the Millennials, and in reality, they are very much the same as these younger Millennials in their attitudes and needs, only taken to a whole other level of intensity." Therefore, I believe it is imperative for Millennials to rise to the occasion, utilizing all the wisdom and character virtues they have inherited from previous generations to fulfill the mission at hand.

As I reminisce about my time spent at Rutgers and Cleveland State, seeking to understand this generation, I ponder what I truly witnessed. As mentioned earlier, there are those who unfairly depict this generation as lazy, narcissistic, entitled, and immature. However, such portrayals are a misrepresentation of who they truly are.

And who are we to judge this generation? As the Bible wisely reminds us, "Why do you look at the speck in your brother's eye, but fail to notice the log in your own eye?" (Matthew 7:3). Before casting judgment, let's engage in self-reflection and introspection.

Certainly, Millennials have their idiosyncrasies, just like every generation before them. However, it's imperative to debunk the myths and misconceptions surrounding them. Beneath the surface lies a generation often misunderstood, hungering for genuine connections, purpose, and an opportunity to prove their mettle. And trust me, they're just warming up.

EMPOWERING MILLENNIALS: Nurturing their Potential and Overcoming Misunderstandings

As we navigate the complexities of intergenerational dynamics, one question stands paramount: How can we work with and help the Millennial Generation, as well as Generation Z to become the best version of themselves, avoiding misunderstandings along the way? We often see them through a distorted lens, assuming they're directionless, entitled, or glued to their phones. But coaching this generation has revealed a fascinating truth: we assume they're lost, aimlessly wandering through life, when in reality, they're locked into a world of untapped potential and a relentless pursuit of purpose.

They are locked into a world that is rapidly evolving, a world that demands adaptability, creativity, and a different kind of focus. Millennials are not lost. They're explorers of a digital frontier, pioneers of a new social landscape. They navigate life with a unique set of skills, honed by the very technology we often accuse them of overusing.

To put it another way, imagine a treasure chest crammed with gold but secured with a complex combination. That's the Millennial mind—a treasure trove of creativity, talent, and drive, just waiting to be unlatched. But the key isn't forcing it open with outdated tools. The key is discovering the unique combination, the code that unlocks their brilliance.

To truly motivate Millennials, we must invest in methods that ignite their creative spark. Their creativity is a superpower. Give them the freedom to experiment, fail, and rise again. Their unconventional thinking can lead to groundbreaking solutions, and they will do and produce far greater than we can imagine. Recognition, for Millennials, isn't just a pat on the back; it's validation, and they crave it. A well-timed shout-out, the chance to lead, even an award strategically placed—these are the fuel that can propel them to even greater heights. Remember, they grew up with participation ribbons and trophies, and that desire for acknowledgment remains deeply ingrained.

Perhaps the most effective way to unlock their full potential and help them become the best they can become is by empowering them to take control of their own destiny. Give them the reins, let them chart their own course. When they feel in control, they'll surprise you with their resourcefulness, resilience, and unwavering drive. Chris Tuff echoes this sentiment: "When you empower Millennials, their work ethic, attitude, and production levels inspired me to become an even better leader."

In closing, I hold firm in my belief that Millennials have been a misunderstood generation—from their coming of age to their current emergence as the next leaders of our society. To this vibrant and capable generation, I offer the following "Waters Words of Wisdom."

The Waters Way - Words of Wisdom

A MESSAGE TO MILLENNIALS: YOU'VE GOT THIS.

1. **Let your faith be your compass.** Millennials, allow God to guide your steps in this world. God's got your back, but you have to trust the map He gives you.

2. **Character is your crown.** Wear it with pride and let it shine in every situation, circumstance, and decision you make.

3. **Your intuition is your secret weapon.** Your insight is your superpower. Don't ignore your instincts. Trust your inner knowing to lead you in the right direction.

4. **Embrace your strengths.** You're a kaleidoscope of talents, so stay true to your authentic self, especially in the areas where your strengths lie. Don't let anyone dim your light.

5. **Intelligence is your shield.** Use your intellect to help you maneuver around any obstacles you face, avoid traps, and always keep learning.

6. **Learn from the past, own your future.** Listen to older folk, they've been around the block and can tell you a thing or two to help you avoid unnecessary errors. But don't let their mistakes become yours. Always remember, "You do not have to lose to learn." (Waters Words of Wisdom)

And remember, Millennials, you have the tools, the intelligence, and the creativity to be the architects of a brighter future. You are poised to become the trailblazers of this new and challenging era. Go out there, claim your place in this world, and lead the way with grace, understanding, and an unwavering belief in yourselves. You are the Millennial Generation—embrace your legacy!

ACKNOWLEDGMENTS

The world we inhabit today is vastly different from the one we knew yesterday. Each generation leaves an indelible mark on the fabric of society, shaping its trajectory and influencing its future. In this book, I have attempted to capture the essence of the Millennial Generation's impact on the profession of basketball, drawing on the insights of many individuals who have generously shared their knowledge and experience.

I cannot possibly thank all the people who have contributed to the creation of this narrative, but I feel compelled to mention a few of them, who have been instrumental in bringing this book to fruition. My wife, Bernadette, who has always been my rock and my fortress, was the first to provide me with valuable information and research to help me understand the makeup of this generation. Thank you, my love, for your unwavering support and guidance.

Next, I must thank our grandchildren (especially our Grand Millennials), Alexia, Emajae, Bryce, Jessica, Gabrielle, Baylee, and Cameron, for providing me with current data and authentic examples of how this generation functions in our society today. I am extremely blessed to have such a close connection with my grandchildren.

I am also very grateful to Jennifer Wainwright, the orchestrator behind the organization and modification of the initial manuscript. Her editing and proofreading were a valuable asset to the formulation of the text.

Another person I would like to acknowledge is Chris Corsl, the sports information director at Rutgers University, for his work in compiling some of the background information and photos regarding some of the players throughout the book. His information was invaluable and greatly appreciated.

I would be remiss not to mention Shannon Wainwright, whose support and guidance throughout the publishing process were crucial in transforming this book from concept to reality.

Additionally, I want to recognize those who, behind the scenes, shared their experiences, life lessons, and memories of past generations. Your contributions helped bridge the gap between eras and enrich the understanding of our collective journey.

Finally, as with everything I produce, including this text, I humbly give honor and glory to my Lord, Jesus Christ. Through His grace and the invaluable contributions of the remarkable individuals who helped make this book a reality, I am eternally grateful.

ABOUT THE AUTHOR

Gary Waters has achieved an impressive array of accomplishments during his 40-plus seasons in college basketball.

In his 21 years as a head coach—five at Kent State, five at Rutgers and 11 at Cleveland State—he amassed 365 wins and led 12 of his 21 teams to postseason tournaments.

One of the most respected coaches in the collegiate game by his peers, he served as a coach for the USA Basketball Men's National Team Trials at the U.S. Olympic Training Center and coached the USA Junior World Championship qualifying team.

HALL OF FAME INDUCTIONS AND AWARDS

Waters has been elected to three Halls of Fame:

- Ferris State Athletic Hall of Fame (2002)

- Kent State Varsity "K" Hall of Fame (2006)

- City of Detroit High School Hall of Fame (September 2019)

In addition, he has received several national awards:

- John Lotz "Barnabas" Award by the Fellowship of Christian Athletes (2010)

- Master Coach Award from the Nations of Coaches (2015)

- Finalist for the Ben Jobe Award (2014 and 2015), presented annually to the top minority coach in college basketball

- President's Medal Award from Cleveland State, the first time a non-faculty member was honored (at the end of his final year before retirement)

PROFESSIONAL ASSOCIATIONS

He is a member of the National Association of Basketball Coaches (NABC), where he served as a member of the NABC Board of Directors, as well as on the NABC Ad Hoc Committee of the NCAA Men's Basketball Tournament Selection.

COACHING CAREER

Kent State (1996-2001)

Waters became head coach at Kent State in 1996, leading the Golden Flashes to a 92-60 record in five seasons. He was one of only three coaches in Mid-American Conference history to earn MAC Coach of the Year honors in successive seasons (1999 & 2000).

Rutgers University (2001-2006)

He moved on to Rutgers University for the 2001-02 season and quickly made an impression. Waters led Rutgers to the National Invitational Tournament in his first season. For his achievements, he was honored as Coach of the Year by the Metropolitan Writers Association of New York.

Cleveland State University (2006-2017)

Waters returned to Northeast Ohio in 2006 when he was named the head coach at Cleveland State University. Over the next 11 years, he guided the Vikings to 194 wins, the most by a head coach in program history.

During his 11-year tenure at Cleveland State:

- All seniors who completed their eligibility in the program earned their degree under his guidance

- The program earned recognition from the NCAA four times for having a program in the top 10 percent of the Academic Progress Rate (APR) among all Division 1 basketball programs (2012, 2013, 2014, and 2015)

PERSONAL BACKGROUND

A native of Detroit, Michigan, Waters was an all-city and all-state performer at Detroit Mackenzie High School. He went on to receive honorable mention All-American, as well as all-conference and all-region honors at Oakland Community College (1969-71). He transferred to Ferris State in 1972, becoming a first team all-league performer and all-district selection. Waters was selected by the Detroit Pistons to participate in the NBA draft trials (1974). Later that year, he was drafted by Spain to play in the international league.

EDUCATION

He earned his bachelor's degree from Ferris State in Business Administration in 1975, and a second bachelor's degree in business education in 1978. The year following his first bachelor's degree, Waters obtained his master's degree in educational administration from Central Michigan in 1976.

PERSONAL LIFE

Gary is married to his high school sweetheart, Bernadette, and they have two children, Sean and Seena Allen, and seven grandchildren. They are both retired and reside in Tampa, Florida.

REFERENCES

Beall, George (November 6, 2017). Article: "8 Key Differences between Gen Z and Millennials." *Huff Post.*

Blanton, Dr. Brad (April 1, 1996). *Radical Honesty: How to Transform Your Life by Telling the Truth.*

Bosche', Gabrielle Jackson (July 20, 2019). *The Millennial Solution: Tapping the Next Generation of Talent.*

Elmore, Tim (2012). *Generation iY: Our Last Chance to Save Their Future.*

Elmore, Tim (2015). *Generation iY: Secrets to Connecting with Today's Teens & Young Adults in the Digital Age.*

Hairms, Julie Lythcott (2015). *How to Raise an Adult: Break Free of the Overparenting Trap and Prepare Your Kid for Success.*

Harris, Malcolm (2017). *Kids These Days: Human Capital and the Making of Millennials.*

Jones, Charlie T., and Tracey C. (April 4, 2017). *A Message to Millennials: What Your Parents Didn't Tell You and Your Employer Needs You to Know.*

Maxwell, John C. (1982). *The Maxwell Leadership Bible: Lessons in Leadership from the Word of God.*

Misztal, Barbara A. (June 2013). *Trust and Modern Society: The Search for the Bases of Social Order.*

Otis, George Jr. (2018). Article: "Revival and the Next Generation – The Emergence of Gen Z and the Reason Millennials are Leaving the Faith."

Rainer, Thom S., & Jess W. (2011). *The Millennials - Connecting to America's Largest Generation.*

Sinek, Simon (2014). *Leaders Eat Last: Why Some Teams Pull Together and Others Don't.*

Tuff, Chris (2019). *The Millennial Whisperer: The Practical, Profit-Focused Playbook for Working with and Motivating the World's Largest Generation.*

Tulgan, Bruce (2016). *Not Everyone Gets a Trophy: How to Manage the Millennials.*

Twenge, Jean M., PhD (2023). *The Real Differences Between Gen Z, Millennials, Gen X, Boomers, and Silents---and What They Mean for America's Future Generations.*